THE

VEGETARIAN

SHABBAT

COOKBOOK

Roberta Kalechofsky
&
Roberta R. Schiff

MICAH PUBLICATIONS, INC

The Vegetarian Shabbat Cookbook(c) Micah Publications, Inc., 2010

ISBN: 978-0-916288-56-3

LCCN: 2010923461

Cover Design by Sara Feldman
Illustrations: Holly Kalisher
Photographs by Jim Feldman and Roberta Schiff
Printed in Canada

MICAH PUBLICATIONS, INC
micahbooks.com

Acknowledgements

Quotations were made available through the Fair Usage Clause of the Copyright Law, and do not necessarily reflect an endorsement of this book.

Shabbat by Karen Fullet-Christensen is published with the author's consent.

Sandy Goodglick, "Friday is always a hectic day...."Dr. Ron Wolfson, "Among the Jews of Syria...." Dr. Ron Wolfson, *Shabbat: The Family Guide to Preparing for and Celebrating the Sabbath,* Jewish Lights Publishing, 2nd edition, 2002

From Rabbi Dov Peretz Elkins, ed. *A Shabbat Reader: Universe of Cosmic Joy,* UAHC Press, 1998: Rabbi J. Sacks, "A Jewish home is a place...." originally from " The Home Where Warmth Rules Over Technology"; Sue Levi Elwell, "Our lives, our Shabbatot have changed...." originally from "A Family Shabbat: Dreams and Reality"; W. Gunter Plaut, "I view the Sabbath as a surcease from....", originally from "The Sabbath As Protest"; Robert Goldenberg, "Already in ancient times...." originally from "The Place of the Sabbath in Rabbinic Literature"; Blu Greenberg, "You would not think of time as having a texture...."originally from "Shabbat"; Ilana Nava Kurshan,"In college I anticipate Shabbat all week...." originally from "Sleeping Through Sunrise"; Rabbi Lawrence Kushner, "We play so that we can go back to work...." originally from "Thinking Sabbath."

Poem, Shabbat, Karen Fullet-Christensen, "Everything Matters: Thinking With A Jewish Mind

"Eggplants" is reproduced with the kind permission of Udi and Jamie Dotan

Special Thanks to Our

Contributors, Helpers, Bottlewashers, and Cooks

Roberta Kalechofsky is a novelist, who wandered into publishing, became a vegetarian, and wandered into writing vegetarian cookbooks. Books written by and published by her can be inspected at www.micahbooks.com. She lives, writes, publishes, and cooks in Massachusetts.

Roberta Schiff lives in Rhinebeck New York where she is very active in the Mid-Hudson Vegetarian Society; she has served as President and has now moved up to Vice President and Events Coordinator. The group advocates a vegan way of life with both community outreach and social events. See their events and more at: www.mhvs.org. Roberta teaches cooking and health education classes. She also performs Stand-Up Comedy.

Robert Kalechofsky is Roberta's husband, a mathematician and philosopher of science, who wandered with his wife into vegetarianism and became the chief tester of her menus, proofreader, critic, and chief consoler.

Holly Kalisher graduated from New York's prestigious Fashion Institute of Technology with a degree in Fashion Illustration and Design. After working for 10 years in New York's fashion district as a Designer, Holly moved to south Florida and has enjoyed a successful career in Interior Design and Graphic Illustration. Holly can be reached at info@HKinteriors.com.

Sara Feldman is an illustrator and landscape painter whose recent work includes small work in pen-and-ink and watercolor on paper, and larger landscapes in acrylic on canvas. Her credits as an artist are numerous: they include seven one-woman shows, a multitude of group shows, illustrator for *The Eternal Flame*, a 1983 prize-winning publication of Congregation Mishkan Tefila in Brookline, MA. Her recent Retrospective covered 50 years of views of America, and. she has used those beautiful warm tones of fruits, vegetables, and flowers for the covers of vegetarian books from Micah Publications.

Jim Feldman is Retired Professor of Electrical and Computer Engineering, the husband of Sara Feldman, and a wonderful baker. Jim went where few challah bakers dare to go. and contributed the wonderful vegan challot, which makes our challot very traditional: Sephardim Jews claim that the bread baked in the Temple did not contain eggs, and they do not bake their challot with eggs.

Kara Abramson lives in Washington, DC, where she works in the human rights field. She previously lived in Chengdu, China, and now is compiling a collection of vegetarian Sichuanese recipes. Her recipes are eggplant sumac stew, Korean Style Barley Salad, White Bean Stew with Caramelized Onions, and Caponata Spread.

Pam Brown has been cooking vegan since 1967 (Impressive!) In 2006 she opened the Garden Cafe in the heart of Woodstock NY. Vegans and vegetarians in the Hudson Valley adore it and many non-veg people enjoy the variety of flavors and the lovely presentations. Cooking classes are taught there too. Reach her at contact@gardenstatecafewoodstock.com.

TABLE OF CONTENTS

Shabbat

A day of prayer:
Museums, a concert, a walk in the park
We ache with the need
To slow our lives down
To make time and room for what's beautiful
Refreshing ourselves
Remembering life should not be defined
By hard news and pain
Struggling to counter the heavy weight
Tipping the balance in favor of joy
Patience and practice
Shift paradigms
Infuse our cells with the trace residue
Moments of pleasure can be a vaccine
An antidote to protect us from
Worry and wheel spins
Of troubling times

Karen   Fullett-Christensen

B'rauchah
Blessing
ברכה

INTRODUCTION

The Significance of Shabbat

The institution of the Sabbath is the most successful social revolution in human history. It reorganized the way people thought about time, about labor, about work, about rest. It has become the most long-lasting revolution; its effects have penetrated every culture on earth. It is so much a part of the human mental outlook and psychic rhythm of time, that even when we don't celebrate it in any particular way, we are conscious that the week is seven days long, and that one day is to be set aside for not working. From the principle of the Sabbath flow our ideas about sabbaticals, holidays, leisure time, even about equality, and that work is not the total definition or occupation of the human being, that all human beings, even slaves--even the animals---must enjoy a respite from toil.

What an extraordinary invention the Sabbath was, and how difficult it must have been for Moses to implement it. Nothing like it had existed anywhere in the world. There is no record of it in Egyptian history. The similarities to the Sabbath which can be traced to Buddhist and Babylonian practice are slender. Buddhist custom allowed priests to take one day a month off "to cleanse their minds" (ca 500 BCE). Babylonian practice allowed kings, magicians and priests to set aside the 49th day to cease judgment and to atone for whatever injustices they might have done. (Interestingly, the king was not to eat food which had been prepared with fire during this time.) Intriguing though these similarities might be, the Shabbat, as conceived by Moses, seems to have been an original idea concerning freedom and the nature of human nature. Its mandate for everyone established an early principle of equality. Its occurrence every seven days made the repetition of that principle habitual and meaningful.

No one had ever heard of such a thing as taking off one day a week to not work. We can gauge the difficulty of having the Sabbath accepted by the sad event of the Hebrew in the desert who was caught violating the Sabbath by gathering wood for fire and was executed for this. (Ex:31:14-15; Num. 15: 32-36) What was the problem? Not merely gathering the firewood. But by instituting the Sabbath, Moses was attempting to create a new consciousness of the human being enunciated by the principle that man does not live by bread alone. He was attempting to snatch out of a void in history a new way of looking at human nature, at labor, by creating a space in time around human consciousness. No one was to build a fire. This was the initial prohibition, but why this prohibition rather than another? We do not know but can speculate whether some dread of the Promethean violation against fire was at work here. In the Greek myth Prometheus was punished for bringing the gift of fire to the human race because fire belonged to the gods. In Greek mythology the gift of fire is the beginning of man as an artificer, the beginning of his long trek towards technological domination of the earth. Without fire, human control over nature would remain forever limited. Did Moses intuit this? Did he seek to limit not only the work week, but human control over nature by prohibiting the use of fire on the Sabbath? Many interpretations of the meaning of the Sabbath exist, but one that has persisted is that observance of the Sabbath should reinstitute our relationship to nature, that our role as artificer and shaper of nature be suspended at least one day a week.

Because no one was to make a fire, and no one was to gather firewood, no one would have an advantage over anyone else. We start as equals before the Shabbat. It is the iron discipline of revolutions that new beginnings, because of the enormous effort it takes to implement them, cannot afford exceptions. The Shabbat was the newest idea that had occurred to the human race since the agricultural revolution and the practice of burying one's dead.

The Pagan world had never heard of anything like it. Jews were admired generally by the pagan working classes but ridiculed by the intelligentsia for not working one day out of seven. As Robert Goldenberg writes in his article, "The Jewish Sabbath In the Roman World Up To The Time of Constantine the Great," "Jews all over the world behaved on the Sabbath in a distinctive way, and this distinctive behavior was visible to their non-Jewish neighbors." Visible, admired--- and ridiculed---but most extraordinarily protected by the Roman emperors. Augustus allowed Jews not to have to appear in court on the Sabbath, "or on the preceding day after the ninth hour." Jews were exempt from having to enter the Roman army on the grounds that they would not fight on the Sabbath. Augustus provided for poor Jews to collect their dole on a day other than the Sabbath. Goldenberg states that, "This recognition of the Jewish Sabbath was actively imposed even on the ostensibly autonomous Greek cities." Explanations for Rome's leniency in this regard are speculative, especially when we consider that many intellectual Romans were hostile to the Sabbath. Seneca regarded the Sabbath "as the enforced waste of one-seventh of a person's life, compulsory inactivity while important matters went unattended." (Goldenberg p. 430); Juvenal attributed the observance of the Sabbath to laziness; Tacitus was hostile to it; Roman writers saw in the idea of the Sabbath the characteristics of the Jew as lazy, idle, shiftless. Roman citizens feared the influence of the Sabbath idea, as non-Jewish workers and slaves were attracted to Judaism because of the Sabbath. Slave owners feared this new idea, which declared the Sabbath was for the slave as well as for the free. The novel idea of freedom for the worker and the slave was here first expressed. Freedom was first tasted on a Shabbat morning, and it seems to have been original in the mind of Moses. The revolution was declared in seven simple words: Honor the Sabbath and Keep It Holy.

> Shabbat is both the result and celebration of the first national liberation struggle. Ruling elites throughout most of recorded history have sought unlimited power to expropriate the labor of others. When there is no limit, when people are forced to work till they drop or drop dead, we have a condition of slavery. Shabbat is the first historical imposition of a limit on the ability of ruling elites to exploit labor.
> *Michael Lerner*

Other than the commandment to honor the Sabbath and not to light fire, cook or work, there were practically no rituals at first associated with the celebration of the day. As Goldenberg writes, "If we examined only the biblical narratives, we would...have to conclude that people knew nothing of the dietary laws or the priestly tithes." (p.432). Meaning and ritual accumulated over the centuries. An early ritual was the gathering of Jews in a synagogue on Shabbat to read a portion of the Torah. The second important addition to the meaning of the Shabbat was that it should be a day of joy, a theme expressed by Isaiah:

> If you refrain from trampling the Sabbath
> From pursuing your affairs on My holy day,
> If you call the Sabbath 'delight,'
> The Lord's holy day 'honored,'
> And if you honor it and go not your ways
> Nor look to your affairs, nor strike bargains--
> Then you can seek favor from the Lord.
> I will set you astride the heights of the earth,
> And let you enjoy the heritage
> of your father Jacob----

Joy, delight, and honor had been added to "cease your work."

The traditional Sabbath food in biblical time was fish. B. Shabbat 118b. records that Rav Judah, the son of R. Samuel bar Shelat, said that Sabbath joy comes through "a meal cooked of beets, and large fish, and heads of garlic." The festive Shabbat table has certainly come a long way.

By the end of the biblical era, the Shabbat was understood as a day of freedom from work, of Torah study, of celebration, of joy enhanced by a special meal. Jews meditated on what it meant to "cease from work," and by the time of the Mishna (200 CE) had evolved a list of thirty-nine categories of don'ts. Goldenberg's analysis of them, as "an artificial list" seems apt. (p. 423). There is no reference to the famous prohibition against buying and selling---though Isaiah's statement had implied it. Aside from the fact that there was a general prohibition against hunting, Romans noted that the Jews did not slaughter their animals on the Sabbath, and that it was not traditional for them to eat meat on the Sabbath, but they noted the eating of fish and beets.

Goldenberg believes that the formulation of the multitudinous prohibitions we associate with the Sabbath did not develop until about 200 CE and that they "revolve around the basic concerns of human civilization." (p.424) Nevertheless, in time the prohibitions became so onerous that rabbis complained that they were "as mountains hanging by a hair." For many Jews, the endless prohibitions countered the sense of joy the Sabbath was intended to evoke.

There is the famous dispute between Jesus and the Pharisees when Jesus pulls out corn from a field to feed his disciples and is accused of violating the Sabbath. His response to this accusation is, "The Sabbath was created for man, not man for the Sabbath." For many Jews, his response constitutes a watershed in the divide between Christians and Jews, but as Goldenberg points out, this observation exists in Proverbs and in rabbinic literature (B. Yoma 85b: "The Sabbath is delivered to you, but you are not delivered to the Sabbath.") Such a statement may seem like common sense, but there has always been a tendency for some Jews to expand prohibitions, such as whether it is permissible to bear arms on the Sabbath. This last issue was settled during the Maccabean wars against Antiochus Epiphanes, when Mattathias declared that "self defense on the Sabbath overrides the prohibition against bearing arms or making war," and that became the halacha.

Traditional Sabbath Food

Among the multitude of do's and don'ts through the ages, however, the don't that has remained consistent is the law against lighting a fire. With this prohibition, we come full circle to that miraculous first Shabbat Moses and the Hebrews celebrated in the desert. Out of this prohibition, a distinctive Jewish cuisine arose, the most famous example of which is the cholent. In this cookbook we honor this prohibition. All our recipes are designed around food that is interesting and delicious, which does not have to be cooked on Shabbat, to creating foods with delicious leftovers for the modern cook, whether she be a busy working woman (or man), a full-time housewife, a part-time housewife, a single person, or part of a large family. This cookbook has recipes and menus for whatever schedule or life pattern you are in.

Also, because of the prohibition against making a fire, lighting candles (tradition puts it at eighteen minutes before sundown) became an important observance---otherwise, prior to modern lighting, we would have had to eat our meals in the dark---which would have diminished the joy of the occasion. For many Jewish families, lighting the candles devolves upon the woman in the household, but more and more families choose to observe it as a family custom, where everyone gathers around the candle lighting. (See Dr. Ron Wolfson: *The Family Guide to Preparing for and Celebrating the Sabbath*.) Sabbath candles are designed to last for the duration of the meal, so that no one need blow them out before going to sleep---which is prohibited. We welcome the Sabbath in with the lighting of the candles. The table is set with our best dishes and wine cups, a kiddush is said over the wine and a motzi over the challah, children are blessed, songs will be sung, stories will be told---and in some families discussions will get heated.

Many families put a tseddekah box in a prominent place for collecting money for charitable purposes. Often this is placed near the candles and money is donated before the lighting. Many families also follow the tradition of washing hands before the meal. Many families encourage guests--even strangers--to be a part of their Shabbat meal. Michael Lerner points out that "bringing guests to your table, is one of the many joys of Shabbat and runs counter to the isolating nuclearization of family life in our world." Around the world Jews have developed a variety of customs to celebrate the Shabbat, but around the world Jews celebrate it in a spirit that unifies them on this single day. Jews everywhere know when the Shabbat arrives, that on this evening they are a universal community at their various tables.

~~~~~~~

Under the threat of global warming, with our awakened understanding of how perilously endangered nature is, the Shabbat has increased its meaning as the day on which we celebrate our relationship with nature, and that we can do that best as vegetarians or vegans.

Vegetarians were the first to call attention to the endangerment of the land, of the food supply, of the immense cruelty to animals inherent in the factory farming system. In a larger context, their protest was against the subversion of land, earth and oceans by the values of the industrial revolution. They were the vanguard of the environmentalists, the localvores, the organic food movement, the return to basic foods stripped of chemicals and pesticides, the spread of farmers' markets, and community farming experiments. They laid the foundation for our interest in natural food and sustainable agriculture. For many vegetarians, their initial impulse was revulsion towards the intensive rearing methods of animals, exemplified by the crated veal, where a baby calf, from first day of birth, is confined for sixteen weeks to a crate not much larger than his own body. His muscles degenerate because he cannot turn around, he lays in urine soaked hay, he licks his own urine and the bars of his crate in a desperate attempt to get the iron into his system of which he has been deprived. The battery hen is another example of the horrors of industrialized agriculture. Caged with five other hens in an area the size of a folded newspaper, in an industrial concrete building, the hen's wings atrophy for lack of space, her beak has been painfully cut off to prevent her pecking at the other hens confined in a space that doesn't allow for escape from each other. Kept in darkness, their reproductive systems regulated by machines, detached from the earth, the sunshine, from the grass, from the sand, from the healing moisture in air, this animal is a freak of nature, detached from the historical/natural processes that had created her. She is not a chicken, nothing God created. She has become dismembered from nature. She is a mutilated industrial creature, and it is a desecration to the Sabbath to place the meat and soup from this chicken on one's lips.

Industrialized farming has brought many other examples of the horrors of the brutal application of the modern values of "efficiency," of the "bottom line" philosophy in marketing. As Jeremy Rifkin writes in *Beyond Beef*

> Modern meat is a testimonial to the utilitarian ethos. The spirit of the animal is ruthlessly repressed and deadened shortly after birth. Cattle are dehorned, castrated, injected with hormones and antibiotics, sprayed with insecticides, placed on a cement slab, and fed grains, sawdust, sludge, and sewage until they reach the appropriate weight....Children of the industrial world have little relationship to or understanding of the animals they incorporate into their bodies three or four times a week.

The question arises how a Jew who observes the Sabbath can celebrate it by eating such meat--or any meat?

The final argument against a meat-based diet---again first enunciated by the vegetarian movement and in Jeremy Rifkin's book, *Beyond Beef,* has now been endorsed by the Union of Concerned Scientists, The Sierra Club, and given its fullest expression in the UN's report on agriculture, "Livestock's Long Shadow," which details livestock's enormous damage to the environment. If the numbers and statistics of the UN's report seem dry, read Rifkin's book.

Moving beyond the beef culture is a revolutionary act, a sign of our willingness to reconstitute ourselves, to make ourselves whole. Restoring nature, resacralizing our relationship to the bovine, and renewing our own being are inseparably linked. They are the essential elements of a new postmodern sensibility, the harbingers of a new earth-centered awareness.

Our danger, latent in our incredible technological evolution from the first Promethean fire to landing on the moon, was prophetically examined by the famous philosopher, Hans Jonas, in his book, *The Imperative of Responsibility: In Search of an Ethics for the Technological Age* (1984). Jonas points out how our domination over nature has placed us in the unprecedented situation of needing a new ethics, one which looks upon the earth as a participant in the ethical climate, where human beings must understand that their responsibility goes beyond the human race. We now apprehend that nature--the environment--is not durable and to be taken for granted, but is in fact vulnerable and possibly perishable. What kind of obligation, he asks, does this new perception place on us? Past moral and ethical concerns grew out of our historical understanding, but technological change occurs with such rapidity, that understanding is swallowed up even as we try to grasp the problem.

No previous ethics had to consider the global condition of human life and the far-off future, even existence, of the race. These now being an issue demands, in brief, a new conception of duties and rights, for which previous ethics and metaphysics provide not even the principles, let alone a ready doctrine. (.Jonas, p. 8)

"The anthropocentric confinement of former ethics no longer holds." Our role of "stewardship" must be re-examined and enlarged. Historic understanding may not be sufficient and reliance on science may be dangerous. New basic principles of ethics--a new vision is required, which

would mean to seek not only the human good of things extrahuman, that is, to extend the recognition of 'ends in themselves' beyond the sphere of man and make the human good include the care for them. No previous ethics (outside of religion) has prepared us for such a role of stewardship--and the dominant, scientific view of nature has prepared us even less. Indeed, that view emphatically denies us all conceptual means to think of nature as something to be honored, having reduced it to the indifference of necessity and accident, and divested it of any dignity of ends. But still, a silent plea for sparing its integrity seems to issue from the threatened plenitude of the living world. (Jonas, p. 8)

The earth's recovery is our responsibility. No one else can do it for us. No other generation has had this responsibility. Vegetarianism is the pledge of what Rifkin calls "a new postmodern sensibility," the pledge to reclaim the earth from the ravages of the industrial revolution. On Shabbat, we honor nature, cease our war against nature, and seek to restore nature.

~~~~~~~~~~~~~

Like Moses, in his final oration, we perceive that we stand on the threshold between life and death, and that to live we must renounce old habits of behavior and thought, and make a new covenant with the earth, one that includes all its creatures. Vegetarianism or veganism is the pledge we make. It is not only symbolic of a new covenant, it is an active way to regenerate the earth by insisting on a new relationship between ourselves and nature. Food is our first bridge between ourselves and the earth. To celebrate the Shabbat with vegetarian food is an historic act of great future portent: it can renew our relationship to nature and, if we implement vegetarianism, renew our relationship to nature itself. It is the first act of recovery for the earth, of an expanding covenant with the earth. Celebrating Shabbat with vegetarian food continues the revolutionary spirit in which the Shabbat was first conceived of as a gift of freedom for human beings. It becomes a gift for all the creatures which God blessed; it restores our harmony with that first miraculous Shabbat when God looked at the created world, found it good, blessed it, and rested on the seventh day.

~~~~~~~~~~~~~

There are many excellent books on the meaning and observance of Shabbat, and we recommend that you consult them if you wish to learn more about its meaning, development and rituals. This is a vegetarian cookbook that can enhance its celebration.

GETTING STARTED

As Shabbat goes from sundown to sundown, many cooks have to consider three meals, the main Shabbat meal on Friday night, Saturday lunch, often after synagogue or temple worship, and Saturday evening, at Havdala. Vegetarian food is often well adapted to keep at room temperature and leftovers from the Friday meal can be served on Saturday or, with some minor adjustments or additions, can be served as a new dish. Read on and discover how.

COOKING TERMS AND INGREDIENTS

We begin with listing and clarifying some basic terms and concepts. For the beginning vegetarian, it's wise to know what these terms are and that, for the most part, they are foods that can be found in local supermarkets. When possible, buy these foods from bulk bins. It's less expensive because you can buy the amount you need; however, one advantage of buying beans or grains in a package is that cooking directions often come with the package---and sometimes recipes as well.

More often now, supermarkets have bulletin board with recipes on them. It's fun to post your own and pick up others from the board. Use the resources you have at hand, bulletin boards, articles in newspapers, directions on packages, and your computer. You can find information about the nutrient values and recipes for almost any basic food you may want to cook with.

There are no animal products in our recipes---as in *The Jewish Vegetarian Year Cookbook*---and no one has ever complained, or even noticed that eggs and dairy are not part of any dessert. Dairy is questionable from the standpoint of health. Cow's milk protein (found in all dairy products) is the leading cause of food allergy in adults and children. Dairy products are sometimes contaminated with E Coli, salmonella, staphylococci, and/or tuberculosis. Pasteurization doesn't always eliminate these microbes.

Dairy is sometimes advertised as nature's most perfect food, yet the majority of African Americans (70%) , Asian Americans (95%), Hispanic Americans (53%), and Native Americans (74%) are lactose intolerant. The protein in dairy may contribute to osteoporosis through causing calcium loss in the urine. Women especially are told to take calcium, particularly after meno-pause, and you should make sure you have a good calcium intake, but it doesn't have to come through meat products. Often, the problem is not the amount of calcium in the body, but that animal products do not allow calcium to metabolize properly and to be properly used by the body. Dairy also can be implicated in the problem of arthritis.

Today there are many substitutes for dairy products: Soy or Rice milk, many fortified with calcium, Vitamin A, and Vitamin B12, vegan cream cheeses, butters, and ice creams. We recommend some brands in this cookbook, but try your own, experiment, and find out what you like.

BEANS: GETTING ACQUAINTED

In our protein obsessed society, one of the most common questions asked a vegetar-ian is "where do you get your protein?" Vegetarians get plenty of protein from a variety of sources, beans being one of them. Beans contain the highest amount of proteins in the plant kingdom, as well as fiber, iron, calcium and other important nutrients. They are low in fat, inexpensive and versatile. Once you learn how to prepare and cook them properly, you will discover how delicious and digestible they are. The more you consume beans, the better your body adjusts.

Unfortunately, Americans do not include enough beans in their diet, and are not acquainted with the great variety of beans, but beans are consumed in great abun-dance all over the rest of the world from South America, Europe and Asia.

Beans can be cooked into soups, loaves, stews, salads, and they can be combined with other grains and vegetables. There are so many varieties of beans from so many different countries, you could eat a different bean every night for a year and still there would be more to try.

Luckily beans are an almost indispensable ingredient for a cholent, especially for a hot cholent for a winter night. It's fun to mix two and three beans in a cholent.

The easiest stovetop way to cook most beans is to soak them overnight in water to cover the beans about two inches. Drain in the morning, rinse in a colander, then bring to a boil and lower heat to a simmer. Cover with a loose fitting top so that steam can escape. There are several steps, but they each take about half a minute: soak, drain, rinse, refill pot to cover beans, bring to a boil, lower flame to simmer, cook until done, usually--2-3 hours. If this seems daunting (which it most assuredly is not) canned beans are available. But check ingredients of canned beans to make sure they aren't high in salt or some other ingredient you don't want. The advantage of soak it, rinse it, cook it yourself is that you have control over the ingredients. And Aduki, lima beans and lentils can be cooked without soaking.

You can experiment cooking beans in a pressure cooker, except for lentils and split peas which should be cooked the usual way. The pressure cooker breaks down the cell walls of the beans, and makes them soft and digestible. Add a small piece of kombu sea vegetable or grated fresh ginger to further help digestion. Even though soaking beans is unnecessary when you pressure cook them, soaking and discarding the water may aid in digestion. Beans and grains need to be chewed thoroughly. When you chew your food rather than bolting it down, an enzyme called ptyalin is released into the saliva that aids in breaking down the fiber and other elements that cause digestion problems.

Many people are afraid of pressure cookers but they are very safe and easy if used properly. They are a wonderful kitchen tool---you can cook vegetables in 2 or 3 minutes, soups in 5 minutes. They have endless uses. Invest in Lorna Sass' book, *Cooking Under Pressure* and discover some uses.

Never eat beans raw. Many are toxic.

COMMONLY USED BEANS

Adjuki, Black Beans, Cannelloni, Fava Beans, Garbanzo (or chick peas), Lentils, Lima, Pinto, Red Kidney Beans, (great for chilis)**, Soy Beans, Tempeh, Tofu, White Beans, small or large**. (Adjuki, lima and lentils do not need to be soaked.) **A visit to a Middle Eastern or Indian store will display a great variety. The newer models of pressure cookers make cooking beans easy and very safe. Beans can be used in soups, salads, loafs, pureed for spreads, and made into bean burgers, which can be served at room temperature with a relish.**

SEITAN

Seitan (pronounced say-tan), or wheat gluten, is not widely known, even among the natural foods community. Seitan is a high protein, cholesterol free, low fat and low calorie food. A four ounce serving of seitan contains approximately 120 calories, 18 grams of protein and 1 gram of fat. Besides being an excellent source of amino acids, it contains Thiamin, Riboflavin, Niacin and Iron. Because it is a rich and satisfying food and an excellent source of protein, it is especially good for people who are trying to eat less meat or make the transition to a vegetarian diet, but people who are allergic to gluten should not eat seitan.

Seitan is an ancient food that has been traditionally eaten in China, Korea, Japan, Russia, the Middle East and many other places around the world for centuries, and by Seventh Day Adventists in America. It is often called "Buddha food" in Chinese restaurants since it is thought to have been developed by Buddhist monks as a meat substitute, or known as kofu in Asian markets.

Seitan is made from whole-wheat flour. Much of the bran and starch is rinsed away leaving the gluten. In its raw form, gluten resembles bread dough, but once it is cooked and seasoned it has the texture and flavor of meat and is sometimes referred to as "wheat meat."
Proper preparation of seitan is a must, but not to worry: Today, there are many varieties of store bought seitan. Like tofu, seitan quickly absorbs all the flavors with which it is combined and, like tofu, it is a highly versatile food that can be prepared in a variety of ways. It lends itself well to stews, stir fries, BBQ, Szechwan cooking, and salads.

SOY FOODS

The soybean has been eaten for thousands of years in Asia. This humble bean has been turned into delicious and highly nutritious foods. Soy foods are the superstars of the plant world. Because of their intense nutritional profile as well as their health giving benefits, soy foods should be at the top of your grocery list (although some people are allergic to soy) According to many studies worldwide, soy products can reduce serum cholesterol, LDL and triglyceride concentrations, and may contribute to a reduced risk of breast, colon, and prostate cancers. Researchers from the National Cancer Institute identified 5 groups of phytochemicals (substances found in plant foods) thought to contain cancer fighting properties. It was found that soy foods contains them all. The isoflavone Genistein has been shown to stop the tumor-forming process by blocking the enzymatic process that forms tumors. Soy foods have also been found to reduce the symptoms of menopause and may have a protective effect from osteoporosis, but these benefits depend upon whatever else is going on in your lifestyle. Obviously, if you smoke, or eat a great deal of meat products, the benefits of soy may be minimal. One should also be cautious about eating too much soy. Some households have "soyified" their kitchens, where almost every product is soy based. Also check to be sure the soy products you buy are not GMO soybeans. Eighty percent of soybeans in the United States unfortunately are GMO's (genetically modified organisms).

There are many types of soy foods, such as tofu, soy milk, soy flour, tamari, miso and tempeh. Delicious frozen desserts and new products appear constantly. Soy foods are used to create many varieties of meat and dairy analogs from tofu hot dogs, soy ice cream to tempeh bacon. They can be purchased already cooked and prepared and simply have to be warmed. You can find these convenience foods in the freezer case in many different natural foods stores or in the dairy case of your supermarket. There are also many cookbooks now that deal exclusively with soy cooking, and can greatly expand your menus. Not all these cookbooks, however, are vegetarian.

The kosher-conscious cook should check for which of these soy products are kosher, for not all are, and everyone should be aware that a processed product, though it may be a soy product, is still a processed product. Check the label to see what else is in the product.

Seitan or tempeh can be added to almost any dish to fill it out, to add protein to the meal, or to transform a cooked vegetable dish, a stew, or a casserole into a sumptuous entrée.

Tempeh--One of the most popular uses of the soybean. Unlike tofu which is made from the milk of the soybean, tempeh is made from the whole bean. It is fermented in a process somewhat similar to cheese and is a traditional food of Indonesia.

SUGARS

In this age of sugar consciousness, the following is a list of different kinds of sugars to choose from in cooking and baking. All these sweeteners produce different results and have different effects on the body, so familiarize yourself with them and experiment with them. Discover their taste and effectiveness.

Agave comes from the agave plant, has a low-glycemic intake and is recommended for anyone who has to cut down on their sugar intake. A wonderful substitute for honey.

Brown Rice Syrup--Malted Grain Syrup is primarily maltose, not sucrose. Rice syrup is 1/3 less sweet than white sugar and loses some of its sweetness in baking, especially in recipes that have a lot of liquid. Best to use in cookies and cakes, added to frosting, or drizzled over strudels and other pastries. A richer and sweeter rice syrup dessert can be had by increasing the volume by 1/2 cup and adjusting the liquid content by 1/2 cup.

Barley Malt is another malted grain sweetener high in complex sugars that has a taste similar to molasses.

Florida Crystals and Organic Sugar and unrefined sugar, all contain 100% sucrose even though they are unrefined.

Fructose is a highly refined sucrose product made from processed corn syrup. Corn syrup is not considered to be a natural product. Unless you can find fructose made from fruit, it is better to avoid it and use products that are unrefined and natural.

Fruit Source ® is made from rice syrup and fruit and is a much milder sweetener. It comes in dry or liquid form and is considered a good sweetener for those on sugar restricted diets.

Stevia is a South American plant that is 30 times sweeter then sugar. It comes in powder and liquid extract form and needs only a few drops to sweeten a dish. This sweetener is great for diabetics, but it takes some experimenting to find out how much to use and how to use it. Experiment with both the liquid form and the powder form for preference.

Sucanat is a dry sweetener, it is made from evaporated cane juice. It is amber colored, like molasses and tastes slightly like molasses.

Maple Syrup can replace sugar in some recipes. **Maple Sugar** is made from dehydrated maple syrup, and can be expensive.

SUGAR, DAIRY, FLOUR SUBSTITUTES & OTHER BAKING INGREDIENTS

Agar: a product of several species of dried seaweeds, known as "agarophytes," used as a vegetarian gelling agent in place of animal-based gelatin. It is tasteless and comes in several forms: bars, flakes and powders. One tablespoon of flakes should be used per cup of liquid (amount of agar may be increased if using an acidic liquid like citrus or pineapple juice). Refer to package instructions if you purchase agar in its powdered or bar forms.

Arrowroot flour ---A thickening starch made from a powdered tropical plant to be used in place of cornstarch.

Flour---Use a combination of whole wheat pastry flour and unbleached white flour. The proportion of wheat to white varies with each recipe depending on what it is. When baking cakes, use whole wheat *pastry* flour and not whole wheat flour. Whole wheat flour is high in protein and is used primarily for bread. All flour can vary somewhat according to its age, humidity in the air and milling process. Therefore, liquid amounts should be added gradually.

Kuzu is a thickening agent, excellent for sauces and grains, for coating vegetables for vegetable tempura. When purchased, it will come in clumps, break up the clumps, store in a tightly sealed jar in your refrigerator.

Milk and dairy products analogs Soy milk or other non-dairy milks can be used instead of dairy milk. Buttermilk can be made by adding 1 Tablespoon of lemon juice or vinegar to 1 cup of soy milk.

SUGAR SUBSTITUTES

Sweetener For 1 cup sugar Liquid reduction
Maple Syrup 3/4 cup 1/8 cup
Organic Sugar--important for vegans because unlike commercial sugar it's not filtered through animal bones.
Agave--treat as honey
Honey 3/4 cup 1/8 cup
Barley Malt/sorghum 1 cup 1/4 cup
Brown Rice Syrup 1 1/2 cup 1/2 cup
Fruit Concentrate 1 1/2 cups 1/2 cup
Sucanat 1 cup n/a
Maple Sugar 2/3 cup n/a

PASTRY/PIE DOUGH

Flaky pastry can be made using a good margarine or grapeseed oil. Keep all ingredients very cold.

Even though healthy ingredients are used, it is still a good idea to limit intake of sugar, refined or unrefined. Refined sugar goes directly to the bloodstream without going through the digestive process. This can create various imbalances as well as an acidic condition. There are many better alternatives to white sugar that are lower in sucrose.

COMMON VARIETIES OF GRAINS

Grains contain many important nutrients as well as much needed carbohydrates, and there is an incredible variety of grains available in the United States.

Human beings have been eating cereal grains for thousands of years and grains are the basic food source for many cultures around the world. However, your grain consumption should be whole grains as opposed to refined products like white rice. Not that eating white rice should be excluded---white rice balances nicely with some strongly flavored foods---but concentration on whole grains and whole foods will give the most benefit. Balance is the essential goal in cooking: balance of flavors, textures, and seasonings as well as nutritional balance. Consuming any particular food group in excess, whether protein or carbohydrates, is bound to have negative results. Each person is different and unique and no one diet is appropriate for everyone, but whole grains are a wonderful basis to any diet, vegetarian or not. They are versatile, easy to use, delicious and inexpensive. Some cooks plan their meals around the chosen grain of the day. Below is an explanation of some of the more common grains:

AMARANTH----Cultivated thousands of years ago by the Aztecs, it has a very tiny round seed and is high in protein, lysine and amino acids. It is usually ground into flour.

BARLEY----One of the earliest known cultivated grains going back to 5000 BCE. Adding some barley to vegetable and bean soups adds flavor, texture and nutrition.

BUCKWHEAT-----Usually known as kasha. Not really a grain, but a herbaceous plant from the same family as sorrel and rhubarb. However, when eaten in the form of groats, it is cooked and treated like a grain. One can make many more versatile dishes with kasha than your Bubbe used to make.

BULGUR----Whole-wheat that has been steamed with its hull removed.

CORN----Once corn is a grain, it can be ground into flour, or into a coarse meal often eaten as polenta or grits.

COUSCOUS----Steamed semolina-couscous comes as whole-wheat or refined.

DURUM WHEAT----The ground endosperm of wheat used for pastas and breads depending on how it is milled—sometimes referred to as Semolina.

HOMINY----Whole, hulled corn which has been processed in a lye bath to remove the bran and germ.

KAMUT----A low gluten wheat product originating in Egypt, usually eaten in bread.

MILLET----A small seed like grain that is high in protein, iron, potassium and calcium. It is such a healthful grain that it is worth developing recipes with it.

OATS--- A highly nutritious grain usually eaten as a cereal or in desserts. Oats can also be served in a more whole form as groats or steel cut.

RICE----There are literally hundreds of varieties of rice which are eaten all around the world. The most common to the United States, whether brown rice or white, is short grain, medium and long grain. However, Basmati, Jasmine and other kinds of rice are becoming increasingly popular. Some cooks also mix rices, such as wild rice with brown rice. The combinations can be interesting. You can also add a vegetarian boullion cube or a TBS of vegall® to the water to give the rice more taste.

RYE----A hardy grain grown since medieval times. It is primarily eaten as a bread flour but can be rolled into flakes and eaten as a cereal.

SPELT----One of the oldest known grains. Spelt contains more protein than wheat, it is high in B complex vitamins and is able to be eaten by some gluten sensitive people.

QUINOA (pronounced keen-wa)----An ancient grain originating with the Incas as their staple food. It contains more protein than any other grain and has a soft, fluffy texture. Quinoa is the only food in the vegetable kingdom that provides all the essential amino acids. The grains are very tiny and must be thoroughly washed. To wash, place a cheesecloth over a strainer, or the little grains will slip through.

WHOLE WHEAT----Hulled wheat kernels that are usually ground into flour. Hard Red Spring Wheat and Hard Red Winter Wheat are primarily used for bread making with the soft wheats used in pastries and other desserts

WILD RICE----Technically wild rice is not rice, but a wild aquatic grass similar to rice. But who cares--it has so much texture.

SALADS: THE ENDLESS POSSIBILITIES

Salads can be far more versatile than most of us know. You can add almost anything to a salad, mix anything in, cooked or roasted vegetables, leftover pasta or beans. Do not get stuck in the iceberg lettuce rut. There are abundant choices of different varieties of lettuce. While romaine is the old standby, there are varieties such as arugula and mesclun mix (usually a blend of baby lettuce and hardy, slightly bitter greens) Combining different types of lettuce and greens adds great interest to a salad. As much as possible, buy organic ingredients for salad, from local farms.

Salads can be composed of many types of food other than greens. Vegetables, cooked and raw, grains, beans, tofu, tempeh and fruits can be put together to make combinations for salads. They can be a light beginning to a meal, a meal in itself for a Saturday lunch, or a fruit salad for a summer Shabbat.

The dressing should match the salad. Avoid drowning delicate leafy greens with heavy, creamy dressings. The dressing should not dominate the salad. A light toss with a flavorful vinaigrette is usually enough. Try a flavored oil such as toasted sesame or any nut oil for a delicious dressing.

SALAD SUGGESTIONS

Balance bitter flavors like radicchio or arugula with a fruity vinaigrette using lemons, limes, oranges or fruit juices instead of vinegar.
Roasted vegetable salads taste great with a dash of balsamic vinegar. Add croutons, toasted nuts, or seeds to add texture and flavor.

Sliced, prepared baked tofu or tempeh available already cooked in most natural food stores is delicious and nutritious tossed in a salad. You get the proteins and the greens together.

For a fancier look, stuff grain, vegetable or bean salads in scooped out tomatoes or avocados.
Always add dressings to leafy salads just before serving, but with a roasted vegetable salad add dressing a little before serving so that the flavors become absorbed.

BASIC GREENS

Even organic greens need to be washed carefully as dirt, grit or occasional garden critters can hide in their leaves. Fill a large bowl or sink with cold water. Remove stems and swish greens around to loosen the dirt. Drain water and repeat until clean. Cut according to the recipe.

For greens like spinach or kale, cook until bright in color with a little bit of crunch to them. Bring enough water to boil to cover the greens, add a 1/2 teaspoon of salt, and then the greens. Taste to see if they are done. .Drain immediately in a colander. They will continue cooking for another minute or so after they are drained. Greens may be immersed in ice water to stop cooking. Red cabbage is great to add to salad. Serve plain or sauté with a little onion and garlic. Or sauté greens, without first cooking, with a bit of garlic in the oil. A great way to use greens is to add them to the last ten minutes of cooking soup.

COMMON GREENS

Bok Choy, Broccoli. Green Cabbage, Chinese Cabbage, Collards, Kale, Mustard Greens, Spinach, Swiss Chard,-red and green varieties, Watercress---enough variety for a lifetime.

LESS COMMON GREENS----Make Their Acquaintance

Broccoli Rabe –sometimes called Rapini, is an Italian green with tight leafy green stalks and little broccoli buds.

Lucinata or black cabbage. It resembles cabbage, but grows in individual leaves and has a dark hue.

SALTS, SPICES, AND SPREADS

Salt comes from a variety of sources in a variety of ways. We use the common iodized salt that pours from the familiar box. Different salts have different amounts of iodine, potassium or sodium, depending upon where they come from, and it is wise to know the differences since many of us consume too much salt. We recommend sea salt in our recipes (even if we don't always say it). Most commercial products have far too much salt in them, and most people use too much salt.

A fun salt to experiment with is "dressing salt." This salt usually comes as flakes and is used to spread *over* your food or salad. You don't cook with it. It is usually quite strong, so a few flakes go far. Serve it in a "salt cellar," a small dish with a little spoon. It is also usually expensive but kosher salt can be used as a dressing salt, and is very affordable.

Another fun thing to do with dressing salt is to mix it with an herb, like thyme or oregano and place on the table in the salt cellar with a small dish of olive oil next to it. Dip your challah in the olive oil, then sprinkle with dressing salt, mixed or not mixed with herbs. This will give your Shabbat table setting an easy elegant touch.

Herbamare ® is a mixture of sea salt and herbs.

Mori-Nu Tofu---A soft custard like tofu that is made from soy isolates. It is best used blended for sauces, egg replacement, desserts and salad dressings. Mori-Nu works well in savory dishes if it is frozen first, defrosted and then used.

Nayonnaise and Vegenaise®---Egg free, cholesterol-free mayonnaise

Earth Balance or Soy Garden are non-dairy buttery tasting vegetable oil products, containing no hydrogenated fat and can be used in many recipes in place of butter. Soy garden has canola oil, Earth balance does not.

Shoya---is a natural soy sauce.

Tamari Soy Sauce---a rich, salty tasting dark brown seasoning made from soybeans that have undergone a fermenting process. The soy sauce that natural foods stores carry are fermented in the traditional way as opposed to most commercial types that are quickly fermented with sugar with caramel flavoring added.

Umeboshi Vinegar----A tangy Japanese vinegar made from pickled green apricots, or the pickled skins of plums. It is not an acidic vinegar, but salty as it is made with a salt brine. A small amount added to whatever you are making really perks up a dish. It is expensive to buy, but a little goes a long way.

Braggs Liquid Aminos---A seasoning made with amino acids that is low in sodium and can be used to replace tamari.

MEASUREMENTS, SERVINGS, AND BAKING NEEDS

There is a joke about a Chinese cook who, when asked how many servings his recipe feeds, answered, "If you are Chinese, ten servings, if you are American, six servings." We don't know your family's or your guests' appetites, and we don't know what else you plan to serve with a dish. Servings are approximate. If a dish is the main dish, the servings must be larger and will feed fewer people. If it is one course among three or four courses, the servings will be smaller and will feed more people. Only you know what you're serving--and to whom. So interpret all serving suggestions for your needs.

All oven temperatures are in Fahrenheit.

Agar Flakes--a clear tasteless blend of seaweeds that can be used instead of jello, available at natural food stores, and supermarkets that carry speciality foods.

Egg Replacer: Read the recipe to determine the purpose of the eggs. Eggs generally have 4 purposes: binding, leavening, adding moisture and/or richness. If a recipe calls for one or two eggs, the purpose is generally for binding and leavening. If no other leavening ingredients are called for, use pureed extra firm Mori-Nu tofu to replace eggs plus extra baking powder or soda (depending on the recipe) for leavening. Replacing the liquid part of the eggs may not be necessary if you are using a liquid sweetener such as maple syrup. However, if you are using a dry sweetener such as Florida Crystals, Sucanot or other unrefined sugar, you will need to add 2 Tablespoons of liquid per egg. Use 1/4 cup of pureed Mori-Nu plus 2 Tablespoons water for each egg, if needed. In most muffin and cookie recipes, the baking powder and/or baking soda provide enough leavening. EnerG® is an egg replacer which can be purchased in health food stores. Follow directions on the box.

Leavening: Baking Powder: you can use baking powder instead of the powdered egg replacer. Generally, you will need 1 even Tablespoon of baking powder for every 2 cups of flour.

Baking soda: Use when needed to balance acidic ingredients. Be sure to whip liquid ingredients well in the mixer or food processor to add air before adding in the dry ingredients.

Sweeteners: maple syrup, maple sugar or rice syrup is often used in our recipes. Use grade B maple syrup for baking. Pick the mildest and avoid the darker varieties of maple syrup for most recipes.

There are also several brands of unrefined sugar we recommend such as Sucanot, Florida Crystals and organic unrefined sugar.

Oven Temperature: Oven temperatures can vary Check whatever you are baking frequently as some ovens bake faster than others, and some ovens have hot spots in different places.

Fat and Fat Substitutes: Canola and olive are good oils to use. Canola has a very mild flavor and is a monounsaturated fat; however we prefer olive oil, and grapeseed oil for baking. Sesame oil has a good Asian flavor, great for sautés. If using olive oil, choose a Virgin olive oil, cold pressed, first press. These can be pricey, so

look for these olive oils when they are on sale or in discount stores. Do not buy any oil in a plastic bottle. Oils should be kept in glass bottles in a cool, dry place.
Fat free baking can result in a gummy texture, but two tablespoons of oil can correct this.

A good margarine, such as Earth Balance is good for anything to which you want to add a buttery flavor. Fruit purees, jams, jellies, pureed Mori-Nu tofu and applesauce will also work as fat substitutes. Pureed prune is another alternative to fat. To make puree prune, place pitted prunes in a pot, add water to cover, bring to a boil, then turn down to simmer for an hour or so, or soak the prunes for about 8 hours. Puree in food processor until creamy, adding extra water to thin.

BRIEF CONVERSION TABLE

1 ounce = 28 grams dry weight, or 29.5 millileter by volume
1 pound = 454 grams
1 teaspoon = 5 milliliter
1 Tablespoon= 15 milliliter
1 cup= .240 liters
1 pint = .470 liters
1 quart= .950- liters
1 stick margarine=.100 grams
1 inch = 2.5 centimeters

OILS AND VINEGARS

Recipes in this cookbook call for olive oil, sesame oil, vegetable oil, safflower oil, and hot Chinese oil (usually as an option). Grape seed oil is recommended for baking.

Vegetable oils are usually canola, safflower, corn, or a mixture of these. Opinion is often divided about their nutritional and taste merits, and the decision is personal. Vegetable oils are not as healthy as olive oil, but lighter in taste, and many people prefer to sauté in a vegetable oil.

Whether sauteéing in vegetable or olive oil, if you are calorie or fat conscious, you can "sweat" your vegetables, by putting a thin layer of oil in the skillet or pot, just enough to cover the bottom, heat a little, then place your vegetables in the pot, mix well to cover vegetables with the oil. After about 2-3 minutes, add a few tablespoons of water to continue cooking the vegetables. Add more water as water boils off, to prevent the vegetables from burning. This method part sautés and part steams the vegetables. The vegetables will taste as if they have been sauteéd, but most of the fat has been left out.

The method works well with onions, green beans, green and red peppers, Brussel sprouts. With green beans, peppers and Brussel sprouts, cover vegetables after water has been added and cook for five to ten minutes, depending on how "limp" or "chewy" you want the vegetable to be.

Olive oil has the greatest nutritional virtues, for it is high in monounsaturated fats, but it can be heavy in taste and it is also often more expensive than vegetable oils. Olive oil aficionados feel about olive oil as wine aficionados feel about wines. Labels of "Extra Virgin, "Virgin, and "Cold Pressed" can be confusing. "Extra Virgin" indicates that the oil was made from the first pressing of the olive and therefore has the fullest flavor. "Cold pressed" means that the oil has not been refined. "Virgin" refers to the second pressing. Olive oil should be stored in a dark bottle. It can be kept for as long as eighteen months, perhaps two years, if it is not exposed to sunlight. Olive oil is expensive, because gathering the olives is a tedious, time-consuming job, since all the olives in an orchard, even on the same tree, do not ripen at the same time. Some caution should be practiced in purchasing olive oil. Because a good quality is expensive, it is sometimes tempting to buy a poor quality oil, but you must be sure you know what this oil has been mixed with.

Sesame oil has an exotic flavor. A few drops added to other oils for stir-fries, or sprinkled over grated carrots transforms a simple dish. It is often used in Asian-cookery. Also gives salad dressings a unique taste.

Hot Chinese oil is not for the faint-hearted, and should be used sparingly, when you want to give sauces or vegetarian gravies a "punch."

The variety of **vinegars** available is astonishing, and each one can impart a distinctive flavor to your salad or marinade. There is apple vinegar, wine vinegar, white balsamic vinegar, dark balsamic vinegar, tarragon vinegar, rice vinegar, brown rice vinegar, and a variety of herbal vinegars.

The quality and price of these vinegars vary a great deal, so you may have to experiment to find out what you like. **Rice vinegar** is nicely mild, but if too mild, add a few drops of wine vinegar to it. You can mix mild vinegars with a few drops of a more acerbic vinegar to satisfy your taste.

HERBS, SEEDS & GREEN THINGS

When the poet John Keats went to medical college in London at the beginning of the nineteenth century, there was an herbal garden attached to his medical school where he not only learned the medicinal uses of herbs, but drew poetic inspiration from them. In his time, herbal gardens were still attached to medical schools and doctors were required to know the uses and values of herbs. Here we are concerned only with herbs as food, but we should recognize their often useful remedial qualities. Like grains and legumes, herbs are making a sensational comeback, adding luster and zest to our meals. They are the great temptresses of the taste buds. A few basil or sage leaves or some dill will transform your soup or salad. But as with vinegars you must make the choice of what to use and how much. The only requirement with herbs is that they be as fresh as possible. Tempting though it may be, don't buy the large size of herbs because it will last too long, and you shouldn't keep herbs more than a few months. Try to buy the whole herb and grind some just before using. (A coffee grinder can work to grind herbs.) Concentrate on your favorite herbs, buy a few of these, buy fresh, grind fresh if possible. If your herbs get a bit aged, quickly sauté to revive flavor---or throw them out.

If you have a little land, even a plot of two feet by two feet, you can plant a few herbs. They require less care than vegetables and will grow in window boxes, on terraces and rooftops in a city, even in a pot in a sunny window. In the midst of winter, you can pluck a basil leaf from a pot on your windowsill and make a salad taste like the outdoors. If it is possible, plant a herb or two in pots or boxes, when they become too expensive to buy.

Herbs can change the nationality of your food. Vegetables become Italian vegetables when cooked with garlic, oregano, or thyme; they become Mexican when cooked with cumin or red pepper; they become Indian when cooked with curry and ginger. You can sprinkle them on baked potatoes, on bread, on rice, on celery ribs, on sliced tomatoes. You can put them in soups and on salads, and vary their taste each time you use a different herb.

Many of our favorite herbs, like coriander, mustard, aniseeds, caraway, fennel, nutmeg, and poppy come from the seeds of plants. Seeds in general have been valued for their health for centuries. Seeds which are not herbs, like sunflower seeds and sesame seeds, are also healthy, high in protein, but also high in fat. These may be sprinkled on foods and in salads, lightly roasted or used plain.

The following is a list of commonly used herbs and suggestions for their use. It is difficult to describe tastes, unless they are distinctively bitter or sweet, so each cook must make the voyage of discovery for him or herself. Notice which herbs are useful for fruits, desserts, in baking, in salads or in soups, and which herbs pair together or work well together so that each brings out the other's flavor. A pinch of salt will also help bring out the flavor--but remember a pinch!

Aniseed imparts a licorice flavor to foods, and is interesting to use on fruit desserts. Try it sparingly at first.

Basil is the beloved herb in pasta and Italian dishes, but is equally good in soups, salads and even on grain dishes, and wonderful on tomatoes.

Bay leaves are used mainly in soups and stews, but should be removed before serving the dish.

Cardamom comes in tiny hard seeds, and can be bought whole or ground. Try it on sliced bananas, baked apples, or sweet potato pudding.

Caraway is often used for decorative purposes, but can be tried in cole slaws, potato salads, and noodle dishes.

Cayenne pepper is used in hot spices, curries, chutneys and chiles.

Chives are a sweeter form of onion or scallion. Nice in soups or chopped into salads.

Cilantro: see Coriander. Never over-use cilantro. Its taste is strong and many people don't like it.

Cinnamon is possibly the most popular spice used in baking. It combines well with nutmeg and/or sugar for toppings on puddings and baked fruits. Also helpful for diabetics. Can be sprinkled on almost anything, even hot oatmeal.

Cloves are also popular in baking and on baked apples and sweet potato puddings, but try them in vegetable stews and chiles for a surprising flavor. Remove before serving.

Coriander is the seed of the cilantro plant, good in soups, bean dishes, curries, and chiles. People who don't like cilantro often like dried coriander.

Cumin is excellent for Mexican dishes. Many cooks like to mix coriander and cumin together.

Curry can be bought ready-made. Curries vary in quality and you should experiment to decide which kind appeals to you. A basic curry can be made from a mixture of two teaspoons each of ground coriander, cumin, and turmeric; 1 teaspoon of ground nutmeg, 1/2 teaspoon of salt, 1/4 teaspoon cayenne pepper and freshly ground black pepper, to taste.

Dill is a favorite herb for salads and soups, and for use in pickling.

Fennel also has a licorice flavor, but not as strong as anise. It is used in baking and on fruit desserts.

Garlic is the darling of Italian and stir fry recipes. Its medicinal values has adherents and opponents. It is related to the onion family and can be sauteed together with onions.

Ginger, like curry, is good in Asian dishes, vegetable stir fries, but also on baked fruit dishes. Use sparingly, since its flavor is usually strong.

Marjoram is similar to oregano, but milder.

Mustard comes in many forms, ground dry, as seeds, and spreadale. The seeds can be used to combine with curries, ginger and cumin. When using in stir fry vegetables, sauté 1 tablespoon of seeds quickly in hot oil until they begin to pop.

Nutmeg combines well with cinnamon, and is good for cooked fruit desserts. Try it sparingly on cooked, pureed broccoli for a surprising flavor.

Oregano has a strong but pleasant taste, and good medicinal value. Like basil, useful in pasta and Italian dishes, but try mixing it in olive oil for dipping challah.

Paprika is useful on stewing onions for flavor and color. Adds a mild, rich taste to stews and vegetables. There is also hot paprika, which should be used cautiously. Look for sweet Hungarian paprika

Parsley is often used--and wasted--as a garnish. It is wonderful in salads and soups, and for making pesto.

Poppy is used to make muhn for hamentashen, but can be used all year round in noodle dishes.

Rosemary is most often used in tomato-based dishes, but try it in breads, muffins, and simple cakes for a different flavor. It can also be used sparingly in salads and soups.

Sage has a strong flavor, usually recommended for soups, but try it cut up finely on salads. Use sparingly.

Saffron is considered to be the world's most expensive herb. Hence, few recipes call for it. But its taste is unforgettable, and experimenting with it can be an adventure.

Tarragon is used most often in salads and in vinegars.

Thyme is a dainty herb, used in Italian recipes, and in tomato stews. Sprinkle it on grains and in bean dishes. Many people prefer crushed thyme, which can be sprinkled like salt, rather than the small leaf.

Make your own herbal mixtures and keep a record of what works.

SHOPPING ORGANICALLY

Organic vegetables spoil more quickly than vegetables preserved with chemicals. You have to learn to time your shopping on a different schedule, perhaps three times a week, instead of once a week when you came home with twelve bags of food which exhausted you to put away. Once you build shopping into your routine, shopping three times a week doesn't take longer than shopping once a week. Make it a habit to stop off at your grocery store on the way home from work or a meeting, or playing tennis, or wherever you are, pick up fresh vegetables and fruits in about twenty minutes and spend six minutes putting them away. This way you can stay on top of current sales of fruits and vegetables of the season. In season, stop often at local farm stands and farmers' markets. You will be buying locally and supporting the farming community. If you buy less when shopping for food, you will waste less, you will tailor your shopping to what you actually need, and save money. Sales are tempting. They're meant to be, but stick to what you need for the week.

~SETTING THE SHABBAT TABLE~

LIGHTING THE CANDLES AT SUNDOWN

FLOWERS, WINE, SHABBAT PRAYER BOOK, SPECIAL DISHES

CHALLAH---WASHING THE HANDS---BLESSINGS

Challah and wine are the crown jewels of the Shabbat dinner table, and challah is the indispensable bread. Many communities have their own special shabbat loaves. But all the traditions of the Shabbat loaf trace their origins to the shewbread that God commanded the priests to place on the shewtable in the Temple.(Num. 15:19-20; Ex. 25:30). While we do not know the original recipe for the shewbread, we know that it did not contain eggs as many modern-day challahs do, for the use of eggs is post-biblical. Contrary to what European Jews believe about challah, eggless challahs are traditional, and Jewish communities such as Syrian Jews do not use eggs in their challah.

In honor of the double portion of manna which God provided for the wandering Israelites, every Shabbat we place two challot on our Shabbat table.
When baking challah, it is obligatory to remove a small amount of dough--a piece about the size of an olive--before shaping the loaves. Just before baking the challot, this little piece is tossed into the hot oven and the baker says the following blessing in memory of the offerings in Temple days:

Blessed are You, Lord our God, Ruler of the universe, Who has sanctified us with your commandments, and has commanded us to separate the challah.

This ceremony is called "taking challah." While both men and women perform it, it is one of the three mitzvoth, along with lighting the sabbath candles and ritual immersion in the mikveh that are special for women.

Following are two recipes for an eggless challah. The first recipe was featured in *The Jewish Vegetarian Year Cookbook*. It was originally prepared for a demonstration in the kitchen of Temple Sinai in Marblehead, Massachusetts by Chelly Goldberg, whose husband Jonas Goldberg was the rabbi of Temple Sinai. Chelly prepared a huge batch earlier in the day to use for a hands-on demonstration of braiding the dough. Sixteen women each braided a small challah, and while the bread baked, Chelly made another batch of dough so that we could see how easily it was done. Meanwhile, the kitchen smelled like heaven. We could hardly wait until the loaves came out of the oven. And what a memorable sight they were! Sixteen golden, tender, fragrant, slightly lopsided, but absolutely delicious challot.

Candles, wine and challah
Weave a wreath of memory

We adapted Chelly's recipe to the vegan kitchen, successfully, using flaxseed and water to replace the eggs. A great tradition is to have a saucer of olive oil spiced with herbs set on the table, and dip the challah into the olive oil. If you have a favorite family recipe for challah, try it this way:

~JIM FELDMAN'S FIRST EGGLESS CHALLAH~

Preheat oven to 350°
2 packages dry yeast
2 cups warm water (105-115°)
1/2 cup sugar, divided
3 Tablespoons flaxseeds
3/4 cup water
6-9 cups unbleached white flour
2 Tablespoons of agave--a substitute for honey
2 teaspoons salt
3 ounces vegetable oil
1/2 teaspoon turmeric
raisins (optional, but include for Rosh Hashanah challah)

In a small bowl, dissolve yeast in 2 cups warm water. (Use a thermometer, if possible. Otherwise, add 1 cup boiling water to 1 cup cold water.) Add 1/4 cup sugar, and allow the yeast to work for about 10 minutes while you prepare the dry ingredients.

Place flaxseeds and water in a blender and blend for about 2 minutes or until the mixture is the consistency of unbeaten egg white. Or grind the seeds in a spice mill or coffee grinder; place ground seeds and water in bowl of food processor and beat to desired consistency.

Place 6 cups flour, salt, remaining sugar and raisins (if using) in a large bowl. Add flaxseed mixture, oil, honey and yeast. Mix until dough forms, adding more flour if needed. Turn the dough out onto a floured surface, flour your hands and knead the dough for about 10 minutes. Add flour as necessary until the dough no longer sticks to the board or your hands.

Oil a deep bowl. Put the dough in it, turning to grease it on all sides. Cover the bowl with a damp cloth or with plastic wrap, and allow to rise for about 1-1/2 hours, or until doubled in bulk.

Punch down and allow to rise a second time. Punch down again and knead briefly. Use a heavy, sharp knife to cut the dough in half. Cover one half while you shape the first loaf.

Oil a baking sheet. Divide one dough ball into three equal parts. Roll each one into a "snake," using a back and forth motion and keeping the dough under the palms of your hands. Each "snake" should be about 16" long. Allow them to rest a few minutes, then pinch the three strands together at one end, braid them, and pinch them together at the other end.

Remove the first loaf to an oiled baking sheet. Shape the second loaf, place it on the baking sheet, and allow the loaves to rise again.

For a crisp crust, brush loaves with cold water before placing in oven. Bake 25-35 minutes. The usual criterion for doneness is that the loaf sounds hollow when rapped on the bottom with your knuckles, or you may insert a thermometer in a crease on the bottom of the bread. It should register 200 degrees . (Continue)

Cool loaves on a cooling rack. Makes 2 large loaves. Freezes well.

Preparation tip: You can make the dough the evening before and refrigerate it after the first or second rising. Extra dough can also be used for dinner rolls.

To form round challot for Rosh Hashana, and the first Shabbat of each month: Divide the dough in two balls. Roll each one into a thick rope and coil the rope upon itself. If you prefer, divide the dough in thirds and make 3 loaves.

You shall take choice flour and bake of it twelve loaves, two-tenths of a measure for each loaf. Place them on the pure table before the Lord in two rows, six to a row. With each row you shall place pure frankincense....
(Lev. 24: 5-7). Numbers 15: 17-21 instructs the Israelites to bake bread and set it aside as a gift to the Lord before entering the Promised Land.

~JIM FELDMAN'S SECOND EGGLESS CHALLAH~

Not for the faint hearted or the kitchen-weary, but a grand experience for those who want to understand the magic of dough. This recipe also comes from Jim Feldman. Trained as a scientist, the methodical process is his. It is involved, but when you are finished the taste of this challah--if made right-- would have made the Temple priests jump with joy, unless they were allergic to high-gluten flour. For those who are, try a rice flour, such as Bob's Red Mill Gluten-Free-All-Purpose Baking Flour.

Preheat 400° for at least half an hour before baking the challah

> 2 packages active dry yeast
> 17 ounces warm water (105-115 °)
> 1/2 cup sugar, divided
> 8 cups (35 oz by weight) high-gluten flour
> ("King Arthur Bread Flour")
> 2 tablespoons of agave
> 2 teaspoons salt
> 3 ounces olive oil
> 1/2 teaspoon turmeric

Dissolve yeast in 20 oz warm water in a large measuring cup. (105–115 °/ 41–46 C) Stir in 1/4 cup sugar, and allow the yeast to work for some minutes while you prepare the dry ingredients. (This step is called *proofing*. The term reflects that yeast was frequently stale or inactive, so you *proved* the activity of the yeast by watching it foam up.)

Place the 8 cups of flour, salt, remaining sugar, and turmeric in a large bowl. Mix the dry ingredients thoroughly. Put half the flour into the bowl, add the other dry ingredients and then the other half of the flour. Mix until the now faint color of the turmeric is uniform through the flour.

Add oil and honey and mix well again. Now add the proofed yeast 10 oz at a time. Mix the flour after each addition of yeast, stirring up from the bottom to insure as much as is possible that all the dry flour gets mixed in. (As soon as the yeast has been added, put a couple of ounces of cool water in the measuring cup, swoosh it around to pick up the yeast remnants and set it aside to be used for adjusting the dough.)

At this point, the consistency of the mix is grainy and not very dough like. It may be too dry in one part and a bit soggy in another. Kneading will cure all of this. During the kneading, a complex chemical process is going on. The yeast is consuming sugars and protein in the mix and growing. As it does this, it modifies the flour mix and turns it into that elastic and rather remarkable substance that we call dough. As the yeast does its work, it requires water (just as you do when you digest food.) Getting the dough to come out with the proper plasticity is a matter of touch. The advantage of hand kneading is that you cannot avoid knowing exactly how the dough feels. Here follows Jim's advice: If you bought good bread flour, you will get a good workout.

Knead the dough for about 10 minutes. Turn the flour mixture out onto a wide flat surface like a counter top, and scrape out all the stuff sticking to the bowl. In front of you will be some very wet globs and some flour that is pretty dry. Keep folding the lump, pressing it out with the heels of your hands and squeezing with your fingers until you have worked the mass into a reasonably uniform ball. Adding a bit of the water with the traces of yeast in it to dry material will help it to mix in and become part of the dough. By this time—about 2 minutes—the ball will have earned the name "dough," but there is still work to be done. Take a brief break and put the empty bowl in the sink and fill it with hot water, and back to the dough.

You must now begin the process of adding *enough* water. As you knead, the dough will become pleasantly plastic but it may seem either extremely stiff or too moist and sticky. Add small amounts of water from the measuring cup to keep the dough from becoming too stiff; keep kneading if it gets too moist. Don't add flour. The yeast will incorporate the excess water. The dough should be just this side of sticky, pleasantly elastic but not too stiff. As you add small amounts of water it will soften; as you knead it will firm up. Keep going for 9 of the 10 minutes. By this time you will be ready for a short break.

Dump out the hot water from the mixing bowl and clean it of any remnants of the original mix. Then rinse and dry it. Now oil the bowl liberally with olive oil. Give your dough that last minute of kneading. Put the dough in the bowl, turning to grease it on all sides and also to make sure that the bowl sides are oiled. Cover the bowl with a damp, clean dish towel. The time to rise is dependent on ambient temperature. The first rise is typically about 3 hours.

Punch the ball down, recover the bowl with the damp towel and allow it to rise a second time before baking. If possible, use a baking stone in the oven, but, in the absence of a stone, a cookie tin works well.

Punch the dough down again and knead briefly. Use a heavy, sharp knife to cut the dough in half. To make two equal loaves, weigh the halves and bring them to the same weight. Typically, by this time each of the two dough balls weighs about 36 ounces. Cover one half while you shape the first loaf.

Divide one dough ball into four equal parts by weight. Squeeze and then roll each one into a "snake," using a back and forth motion and keeping the dough under the palms of your hands. Each "snake" should be about 16" long. Pinch the strands together at one end, braid them, and pinch them together at the other end. [The braiding formula that Jim uses—and as this formula comes from a male who never braided his daughter's hair, you may have a better way—is to number the strands from left to right: **ABCD**. **A** goes over **C** and then twist **A & C** half a turn. Now the strands are arranged **BACD** with a half twist of **AC**. Do the mirror operation from the right. **D** over two strands and half a twist with A to make **BADC**. Note that the two inside strands have moved to the outside. Repeat the same operations, left and then right, until the loaf is finished. At this point, this high–gluten bread dough will seem to have a mind of its own. It will refuse to stay well bonded at the ends. The cure is squeeze the strand ends together; then, grabbing the ends between the first and third joints of your fingers, tuck the ends of the strands under the end of the loaf and press up. That seems to contain it. Finally, finish by gently rolling the completed loaf on the flat surface (counter top) to get a smooth, compact loaf.

Repeat with the second loaf. Allow them to rise for a few minutes.

Now comes a choice. If you want poppy seeds on your challah, you must use some binder to hold them on the bread. (If you don't want poppy seeds, skip to the next paragraph.) A vegan binder is to take a tablespoon of flax seed and two ounces of water. Mix in a blender at high speed until the mixture gets milky. Then brush it on the loaves and sprinkle heavily with poppy seeds. [Poppy seeds can be purchased inexpensively in bulk over the internet.] Remember that the loaves will triple in size so that dense spread of seeds will thin out by quite a bit. Now to the baking.

Using a baker's peel (large spatula) with a thin coating of corn meal as a lubricant, place loaves on the stone or baking sheet. Bake for 36 minutes. While baking, about every 5 to 10 minutes, spray the walls of the oven and the bread with water to increase humidity in the oven and thus get a crisper crust. If the oven is not entirely uniform in temperature, reverse the breads at about 18 minutes.

When you take the loaves out of the oven, before turning off the oven, tap the bottom of each loaf to be sure that you get a hollow sound all along the loaf. If so, you are done; if not, put them in for another 5 minutes. Leave the loaves on a drying rack for at least half an hour to allow moisture to escape.

You're done!

Sources on the internet:

>   http://shop.bakerscatalogue.com/items/ [general baking supplies]
>
>   http://www.americanspice.com [seeds in bulk]

~OLIVE OIL FOR DIPPING CHALLAH~

This is a wonderful tradition: Place a bowl or two with olive oil on the table (depending on how many guests you have). The olive oil can be seasoned in a variety of ways: with oregano, sesame seeds, or hot chile pepper (if you're up for it). Favorite herbs for oil are rosemary and sage. Small dishes of tapenade * can be served along with the oil. Dip a piece of challah lightly into the oil, spread with tapenade, or see recipe for herb mixture under Salts, Herbs and Spices.

2 cups olive oil, or enough for guests
8-12 cloves garlic (may be roasted beforehand)
2 red peppers, deribbed, cut in 2" chunks
(may be roasted beforehand, or steamed for about 2-3 minutes)

* **Tapenade** is a spread made mainly of finely chopped olives and some olive oil. Sometimes chopped roasted red pepper is added.

~~ *ENTREES* ~~

Shabbat has long been identified with cholent, but this is largely an identification with Eastern European Jews. From what we know of writings during the Roman times, Jews throughout the Roman Empire ate fish for their Shabbat meal. Food traditions, like most traditions, are usually regional, not international. Nevertheless, the cholent deserves a special place because it still evokes nostalgic memories of children or mothers carrying large pots of cholent to the neighborhood's local baker to leave in his oven to bake. The following biographical essay evokes just such a memory from a Jewish immigrant neighborhood in the early part of the twentieth century. It was sent to us via email.

"On a late Friday afternoon, during the 1920's, a child of about ten can be seen carrying a covered roasting pan through the late afternoon streets of the lower East Side of Manhattan. Her mother has given her instructions to carry it directly to the local baker, and not to set the pan down or stop to play, or undo the string tied around the cholent. The baker, having banked his coal-fired oven for the Shabbat, would place the roasting pan along with the various covered pots and roasting pans of his other customers within. Initials and names were marked on the surface with a mixture of flour and water which, when baked, became deep brown. The lid was sealed with the same flour-water mixture. This ensured that the flavors of the Shabbat braise within, that was to slowly cook for the next twenty-four hours, did not escape.

The baker charged a few pennies for this service. The string was to ensure that a careless child wouldn't jiggle the cover and break the flour seal. The child was my mother. The pot that was carried to the baker contained the ingredients for the quintessential European Jewish dish, the cholent."

Food, diet, and cuisine often reflect political situations.

Most Americans think that chopped liver, pastrami sandwiches, bagels and lox are "Jewish foods," but these are food of northeastern Europe, which were adapted to fit the Jewish kitchen by Jews of those areas. As Jews from northeastern Europe travelled and settled in different parts of the world, these foods stayed with them. Sephardic Jews and Jews from India would not recognize these foods as "Jewish" food.

The term "Sephardic Jews" refer to Jews who came from Mediterranean countries, Spain, Portugal, Turkey, sometimes Egypt. Mizrahi Jews come from Middle Eastern countries like Syria, Iraq, Iran (the Persia of Queen Esther's time. Often the terms, Sephardic and Mizrahi are blended.) Many Jews have lived in these countries since the dispersion after the fall of the Temple in 70 CE, and even before. Babylonian Jews date their civilization back to the fall of the first Temple. Sephardic Jews were among the oldest citizens in these Middle Eastern countries until they were sent into exile from these countries in the 1950s. Other Jews who had settled in Spain and Portugal, fled during the Inquisition and their expulsion in 1492. Though Sephardic Jews emigrated to all parts of the world, including the New World, most Sephardim settled around the Mediterranean and intermingled with other Jewish communities already settled there.

Just as bagels, lox, chopped liver, etc. are thought of as Jewish food, so is felafel, but the felafel is a native Middle Eastern dish, along with hummus, stuffed grape leaves, and babaganouj, long eaten by the Arab populations in the Middle East, now eaten as popular snack foods by Jews and others everywhere, and thought of as "Jewish food."

Like music, food travels throughout cultures. It is a great cultural mixer and we often don't know where a recipe or a tune first began. Appetites, like our senses, are ubiquitous, and reach out for everything that is enjoyable to the ear and to the stomach. Immigration is one of the greatest facts of history, and immigrants are one of the greatest forces for spreading cultures.

All of which begs the question: is there really such a thing as "Jewish food"? There is the Passover meal where the meal is described in the Bible and the Talmud, though even here we find variations based on the cultural backgrounds of the participants. There are dozens of varieties of charoshes, and even the matzoh has undergone gourmet changes.

But there is one meal beside the Passover meal that observant Jews share around the world, and this is the Shabbat meal. The ingredients of the meals change from country to country, and from era to era, but the biblical injunction not to labor on the Shabbat--while the desire to produce a meal filled with joy remains the same. Today's traditional cholent is made at home. The stew pot sits over a low flame on a metal flame tamer, a flat piece of metal that spreads the heat slowly and evenly, or in a low oven (200°). For some the crock pot or slow cooker or the dehydrator may do the same job more efficiently without the need to leave home. The rationale behind the dehydrator is that slow cooking doesn't destroy the precious enzymes in the food---one of our imperiled nutrients. Our email correspondent continues:

"Just as there was no such thing as the "unique" cholent, but endless variations, so vegetarian cholents are a variation suitable for the modern diet. National differences existed a hundred years ago, and exist now. Russian Jews substituted potatoes for beans. In Galicia, they added barley and calf's leg. A cholent could be a simple noodle pudding or potato pudding, called a "kugel" in Yiddish. In parts of Germany, apples and matzoh were added to the noodles. Along the Polish-Austrian border raisins and sugar, and sometimes cheese, were added. Therefore a cholent wasn't always a cholent and although Yiddish was spoken from Germany to France, the word "cholent" wasn't used. Instead, the term "schalet" was used in these areas--a word found in the Larousse Gastronomique. Heinrich Heine, the famous German Jewish poet, parodied Schiller's "Ode to Joy" in "Prinzessin Sabbat" (Princess Sabbath), one of his "Hebrew melodies." In this poem he sings a paean to schalet.

"The word "cholent" derives from the Vulgar Latin 'calente,' which in turn gives us the Spanish 'caliente' as well as the Catalan 'calent,' and French 'chaud' from the old French 'chauld.' They all mean "hot.""

"The tradition of allowing the meal to cook over the Sabbath comes from a phrase in the Commentaries (the collection of ancient Jewish law which, with the Mishna, make up the Talmud.) In preparation for the Sabbath, the phrase 'tamen et hachamin, or "hide, or bury the hot things," has come to mean "cover the hot food." In every language used where Jews lived, Yiddish, Jewish/Arabic or the Arabic spoken in Calcutta, Baghdad or Ethiopia, the two basic words of the phrase refer not to the food, but to the method used in cooking, suggesting that the important element for Shabbat food was the preparation, not the ingredients.

"The word for "hot" in Hebrew is 'chamin' and it has become the name of this Sabbath food itself. Calcutta Jews know it as 'hameen.' The other word, "hidden" is found everywhere in the Middle East in different forms of the same word: tfina, adafina, dfina, adefina. They all mean "covered" or "buried."

The idea of unattended cooking on the Sabbath produced a popular Spanish dish, the 'cocido madrileno,' or boiled dinner with chick peas. It is known to Spanish Jews as 'adafina.' Probably emigres spread the knowledge of this dish, because we find a similar dish in the Jewish populations of Cuba and Egypt. Both groups called it 'dfina.' When Jewish *pied noirs* came to France after Algerian independence, they brought adafina with them. French-speaking Jews shortened the term to 'daf.' In Morocco, the dish is called 'sefrina' or 'schina,' which means hot.

These terms and the concept of the hot, covered dish are post-biblical, and therefore we do not find them among Ethiopian Jews, who were separated from the main body of Jews before the Talmudic era."

Today, cooking has returned to slow cooking and eating has returned to slow eating. Both are the essence of the Shabbat meal.

We begin the section of entrées with cholents because it is such a well known traditional dish for Shabbat, and it is a good dish if you are going to serve many people. All cholents have basic ingredients: beans, potatoes, carrots, onions, garlic. They are meant to be hardy and slow cooking. Wine or sherry can be added to many cholents for a richer taste. Notice other variations.

~MIXED-BEAN CHOLENT WITH TEMPEH~

Nowadays one can find many recipes on the internet. The next two cholents are inspired by Archives Homepage, Cholent index. In the world of cholents, beans are basic, and almost any combination of beans will do.

Preparation: Rinse beans, then soak beans overnight in a large pot with two-three inches of water to cover.
Heat oven 200 $^\circ$

1/2 cup pinto beans
1/2 cup white navy beans
1/2 cup lima beans
2 Tablespoons oil
1 very large onion, chopped
3 cloves garlic
3/4 cup barley
3 large potatoes, cut in chunks
1 teaspoon paprika
2 bay leaves
salt & pepper to taste

Heat oil in a 4 quart pot, sauté onions and garlic together until onions are wilted and transparent. Add the barley and beans to the onions. Cover with water by two-three inches, add bay leaf, salt, pepper and paprika. Bring to boil and cook 30 minutes over a low flame. Add potatoes (peeling is optional) and cook 30 more minutes.
Place the cholent in a slow cooker overnight or in oven for at least 8 hours. Sauté strips of lightly marinated tempeh. Add to cholent 1/2 hour before cooking is done. At this time, remove the bay leaves.
Serves 10

Variations: Add two small cans of no-salt tomato sauce or 1 can of tomato paste pureéd with 3-4 tablespoons of water. Add 1 cup of cauliflower flowerets, or handful of dried cranberries for color and taste.

~VEGETARIAN STEW CHOLENT~

This recipe also comes from the Archives homepage, cholent index. The original source was *Joy of Cooking* by Wendy Baker. The original recipe included the option of 6 eggs in their shells. We also substituted portobello mushrooms for shitake mushrooms, because portobellos yield a heartier taste.

Preparation: Soak soy beans ahead.

> 1/2 cup of dried soybeans, soaked
> 4 large portobellos
> 1-3 Tablespoons olive oil
> 3 large carrots, or 1 pound regular carrots, peeled, cut into chunks
> 6 medium size unpeeled potatoes cut into chunks
> 1 large onion cut into chunks
> 1 large green pepper
> 4 ribs of celery, cut into bite size chunks
> 3 cloves of garlic, chopped
> 18 ounce can of tomato sauce
> 1/2 cup dry wine, or dry sherry
> 3 teaspoons of vegetal or vegetarian soup powder
> 12 cloves
> 10 peppercorns
> salt and freshly ground pepper to taste
> 1/2 cup water, if needed

Chop 1/3 of the onion, 1/3 of the green pepper and the garlic together
Heat oil in a small skillet, sauté the chopped onions, green pepper and garlic until lightly browned.
Oil a larger skillet, add carrots and potatoes on the bottom, then the soaked soy beans, then the rest of the vegetables, then the portobellos.
Add seasonings, sautéed vegetables. Add wine or sherry, then water if needed. Remember that the vegetables will produce liquid themselves.
Cover tightly on low heat, cook for about one hour before Shabbat begins, until potatoes are soft, but not mushy. Can be served at room temperature for Saturday lunch.
Serves 6

~CURRY CHOLENT~

A great variation on cholent, with a spicy Middle Eastern flavor to it, inspired by Gabi Shahar (gabi@salata.com). This recipe is good for an adventurous crowd. Consider a Shabbat party with this dish. Make it as hot or as mild as you wish. We have simplified some of the steps, but you can check on the original recipes at Archives Homepage, Cholent Index. Start this dish Thursday night because it cooks in the oven for at least ten hours.

3 Tablespoons olive oil
2 medium size onions chopped
2 cloves of garlic, chopped
1 inch of fresh ginger grated, or 1 teaspoon of commercial ginger
4 Tablespoons of curry powder
1 large can crushed tomatoes. Keep juice
1 cup vegan sour cream
6 potatoes, scrubbed and cut in chunks (peeling is not necessary)
2 yams or sweet potatoes, scrubbed and cut in chunks
2 carrots, scrubbed
1/2 pound of brown beans
salt and pepper to taste

Heat oven to 220 °

Ahead: Cover beans with water, bring to a boil. Boil 3 minutes, remove from fire, let them rest for 2 hours. Drain and rinse.

Heat oil in a large pot suitable for oven. Sauté chopped onions, garlic and ginger over low flame, 10-15 minutes. Add curry, and sauté another 2 minutes. Add tomatoes, with juice from the can, cover, cook ten minutes, stir occasionally. Add vegan sour cream, salt and pepper to taste. Mix well.

Add potatoes, yams, carrots and beans. Cover with boiling water 1/2 inch over the top. Cover with a fitting lid, and place in oven for about ten hours.

Serves 12

~LEEK, EGGPLANT, AND SQUASH CHOLENT~

This combination may sound eccentric, but it works. Use an acorn squash.
Bake the squash in advance.

Oil
3 medium leeks, well washed
1 medium size eggplant, scrub skin, and cut into
large chunks
3 garlic chopped cloves
2 large potatoes, scrubbed and cut into chunks
1 eight ounce can of tomato sauce or crushed tomatoes
1-1/2 cups squash

Oil bottom of large kettle and heat
Chop leeks in food processor, stir in kettle for 3-5 minutes
Add eggplant chunks and garlic cloves to leeks in the kettle, mix well
Add potatoes and tomato sauce or crushed tomatoes. Cover and cook for 40
minutes or until potatoes are soft
Mash squash, but not too fine, leave it kind of chunky
Add squash, mix, heat well, serve

Serves 5-6

"The official beginning of the Shabbat is at sunset
the previous evening, and a notice in the paper
tells exactly what time it is. After you've been
through a few of them you can see why. They
don't just close the stores; they shut down the
whole city. Now that I'm used to it, I'm all for it
and think if they'd shut down the whole world
one day a week, we wouldn't be in the mess
we're in."

(Reporter for *Vogue,* July, 1969, p.11)

~EGGPLANT RATATOUILLE CHOLENT~

Essay on A Recipe

Sometimes a cholent is a stew, sometimes a ratatouille is a cholent.

The following dish was taken from a recipe by M.F.K. Fisher, considered to be America's premier writer on food. She boasts that the recipe was taken from another recipe in the book, "Long Ago in France." Our changes show how you can work with almost any recipe to suit your taste.

What fascinates about this recipe is that M.F.K. Fisher, in loyalty to cookbook writers from long ago, refuses to give amounts for each ingredient, or the size of the pot she is cooking with. Remember when our grandmothers said, "I throw in a handful of this and a small amount of that until it tastes right to me." That's how it used to be done. But our age is addicted to numbers, and quantities have to be specified for every ingredient, though every family is different and every recipe should be altered to suit your tongue, your pocketbook, your allergies, your family's needs, etc. Here is how M.F.K. Fischer tells you to cook this sumptuous dish (parenthetic remarks are ours.)

"The ingredients were and still are eggplant unpeeled, and onions, garlic, green peppers, red peppers (if they are procurable), plenty of ripe peeled tomatoes (I never peel tomatoes--too fussy for me), and some good olive oil. Proportions are impossible to fix firmly, since everything changes in size and flavor, but perhaps there should be three parts of eggplant, and/or squash, to two of tomatoes and one each of the peppers and the onions and the garlic. I really cannot say (notice the candor).

"Everything is sliced, cubed, chopped, minced, and except for the tomatoes, is put into the pot...when there is less than no room (notice the odd wording), the tomatoes are cubed or sliced generously across the top, and the lid is pressed down ruthlessly (a typical Fisher adjective). When the lid is taken off (when? no time is given), a generous amount of olive oil must be trickled

~39~

over the pot to seep down. to the bottom of the pot. Then the lid is put on again. It may not quite fit, but it will soon drop into place. The whole pot goes into a gentle oven (at last! at a number. Fisher recommends 300°), for as long as one wishes to leave it there, five or six hours (how utterly insouciant!). It should be stirred up from the bottom with a long spoon every couple of hours. It will be soup for a time and that is when it makes a delicious nourishing meal served generously over a slice of toasted French bread (substitute challah).... Gradually it becomes solid, as the air fills with rich waftings which make neighbors sniff and smile. When it reaches the right texture to be eaten as one wishes, even with a fork, the lid can stay off. (Here Fisher suggests that shrimp or sausages cooked in beer or wine be added. We suggest grilled tofu triangles, and that a cup of wine added to the ratatouille would not be a bad idea.) Or it can simply be left in a turned-off oven, to be chilled later for probably the best so-called ratatouille ever eaten." Yes, but how many will it serve? We don't know how big the appetites of your guests are, or what else you are serving with this, but here's a guess: **8-12**

~BROCCOLI LOAF~

For those of us who wish to serve something other than a cholent or a dish resembling a cholent, Ethel Goralnick, a seasoned cook who has written many articles, asserts, "People unfortunately want recipes, but it is best to be free of them and just have the guidelines and to taste." But here are some suggestions from her, laid out in modern recipe style: Broccoli is so healthy, that any way you eat it is good. Prepare this loaf for a winter Shabbat and bake potatoes and squash with it, but make enough for the next day because broccoli loaf at room temperature might be just the thing for a Shabbat afternoon lunch.

Heat oven 375°

3 cups of broccoli florets, steamed and pureed in food processor
1/2 cup wheat germ
1/4 cup nutritional yeast
1/2 cup chopped onions or scallion
1/4 cup parsley
1/2 cup vegan cheddar cheese
pinch of salt
1 Tablespoon of seasoning
  sprinkle top with paprika
Optional: pinch of nutmeg on top.

Oil small loaf pan. Mix all ingredients together. Bake 40 minutes or until top browns, and there you are. Could anything be easier?

Serves 4-5
Note: Nutritional yeast is light and flaky, rich in Vitamin B12, and adds a cheese flavor---can be used in place of Parmesan cheese.

~CURRIED EGGPLANT, CAULIFLOWER, AND POTATOES~

Steamed eggplant has the virtues that it cooks quickly and is low in calories, but its bland taste often leaves foodies unimpressed. Here are two recipes that will change your mind. Like tofu, eggplant is a great mixer and absorbs spices and flavors. One problem with eggplant is that the best eggplant dishes are usually fried and soak up lots of oil, but following are two eggplant dishes that can be steamed and are delicious. The steamed eggplant gives the cauliflower a creamy texture. This is an easy dish to make, but timing is important. So have your ingredients ready in advance to coordinate the cooking. However, this dish is not suitable for the following day, because cold steamed eggplant is not appealing.

2 cups of large cubes of eggplant (leave skin on)
3 cups of cauliflower flowerets
3 medium size potatoes, cut in large cubes
1 Tablespoon of mild curry powder
1 teaspoon ginger or 1/2 teaspoon fresh grated ginger
pinch of salt
oil for skillet

Put eggplant and cauliflower in double boiler and steam until eggplant is soft, but not mushy.
Boil potatoes in water to cover until soft, but firm
Heat oil in skillet, add curry, ginger, and pinch of salt
Add eggplant, cauliflower and potatoes, cover well with curried oil
Cook for additional five or six minutes. If vegetables stick, add 1/4 cup water or more to prevent vegetables from sticking.

Serves 4-5.

Tip: Place potatoes in bottom of double boiler and eggplant in top of double boiler, and cook both together. Saves pots and time.

~SWEET AND SOUR TEMPEH~

There is a special taste in the combination of sweet and sour that many people adore. This is an interesting version of this taste.

> 1 pound tempeh, cubed (Soyboy brand, if possible.)
> Sesame oil for sauteing
> 1 medium onion diced (Vidalia or red is good)
> 2 Tablespoons fresh, grated ginger
> 1 red and one yellow or orange pepper in medium dice
> 1 cup green beans ends trimmed and halved
> 2 Tablespoons arrowroot or kuzu powder dissolved
> in 1 1/4 cups water
> 5 Tablespoons tamari
> 3 Tablespoons apple cider vinegar
> 1 Tablespoon light miso
> 7 ounces apricot preserves (use the fruit sweetened kind)
> 2-3 Tablespoons black sesame seeds

Steam the tempeh for about ten minutes then marinate it in a mixture of tamari, olive oil, and a bit of leftover red wine. (marinating is optional, but it gives the tempeh a nice taste.)

Heat 3 Tablespoons water in a large skillet. Add onions and sauté until a bit brown (you can add small amounts of water a few times)

Add the ginger, peppers, sauté a bit more. Meanwhile sauté the tempeh cubes in another skillet until just browned. Add the green beans to the other vegetables, then add the tempeh. Add the vinegar, tamari, miso, preserves and the arrowroot dissolved in the water. Stir constantly for a few minutes until the sauce is smooth. Hold off on the green beans, if not serving right away. A few red pepper flakes will add intensity for the brave-of-heart. Just before serving sprinkle the sesame seeds on top. Serve with jasmine rice.

Serves 6

~GINGERED EGGPLANT AND~
~POTATOES IN GINGER SAUCE~

This recipe is similar to curried eggplant, cauliflower and potatoes. The dish can be turned into a delicious curried vegetable and fruit dish. It is also easy to expand this dish to serve 8, if you add the recommended fruits. If you want the dish to have a fruity taste, eliminate the potatoes, especially if you are serving the dish over rice, barley, or millet

1 medium eggplant, cut in cubes, leave skin on
3 medium potatoes, cut in cubes
1/2 cup raisins

Place potatoes in boiling water in the bottom half of a double boiler steamer. Place eggplant cubes in top of steamer, cover and cook both. In the mean-time, prepare the curry.

SAUCE
1/4 cup soy sauce
1 Tablespoon mustard seeds
1-1/2 teaspoons ginger
oil for skillet

Heat oil in skillet on medium heat, and place mustard seeds in skillet to cook until they pop. Be careful because sometimes mustard seeds can pop hard enough to hit your face. They also char easily, so make sure heat is not too high. When seeds have popped, add ginger, curry and pinch of salt. Drain and remove potatoes and mix in well to coat with curry mixture in skillet.
Serves 4-5

Variations: Use zucchini instead of eggplant or with eggplant for a more textured vegetable dish. Add steamed apricots to raisins or instead of raisins, add slices of granny smith apple, and serve over rice or rice barley. Baked or toasted tofu cubes can also be added. If you add the variations, this dish will serve 6-8.
Tip: This sauce, without the fruit additions, can also be used as a sauce for pasta. Drain pasta, add to skillet with the sauce, mix and cover well.

~THE LONG AND SHORT OF STROGANOFFS~

This is a dish that can be as versatile as your imagination. It can be made with a variety of ingredients, and be as simple or as complex as you like. The beauty of this dish is that you can make the stroganoff with all kinds of vegetables or browned tofu. It can hardly be ruined, but stroganoffs are best eaten on the day they are made. Below is a favorite mixture.

Basic Recipe

1 Tablespoon of olive oil to oil skillet
1 large onion---sauteed
1/2 head cauliflower, steamed to semi softness
1 large cup halved mushrooms
pinch salt
1 teaspoon ginger, or 1/2 teaspoon of fresh ginger
1 Tablespoon curry powder
1 Tablespoon Hungarian paprika
2/3 cup vegan sour cream

Sauté onions, mix with ginger and curry powders
Add halved mushrooms, add steamed cauliflower. Mix well.
Add vegan sour cream just before removing from heat, mix again thoroughly.
Add more ginger and curry to taste, mix.

Serve over flat noodles or rice.

Variation: Add or substitute for the cauliflower marinated and browned large cubed tofu pieces. Leave a few minutes extra for this, remove the tofu pieces to a hot plate, and add back into skillet after the onions have been sautéed, or after the mushrooms have softened.

Serves 6. Recipe can be increased to serve 8 or 10.

~CAULIFLOWER PAPRIKA STROGANOFF~

Horseradish is often overlooked as a great condiment to food. This recipe will amaze you with what a little horseradish can do. It's simple to make, but tastes best when freshly made.

2 Tablespoons olive oil
1 large cup chopped onions
1-1/2 teaspoons horseradish
1 large cup vegan sour cream
2-3 teaspoons paprika
1 large head cauliflower

Separate cauliflower into flowerets and steam for about 7 minutes, until semi soft.
Heat olive oil in a large skillet. Sauté chopped onions until lucent.
Sprinkle in the flour, mix thoroughly, cooking over low heat.
Add the horseradish and vegan sour cream. Continue to mix for about 2-3 minutes.
Add the cauliflower to this mixture.

Add paprika, mix everything well. Cook for another five minutes over low heat. Taste. You may want to add a little more horseradish. It's best to test this as you go along. Cover to keep warm.

Serve over rice or rice noodles. Goes well with a green salad.

Serves 6 hearty portions

~THE ENDLESSLY EXPANDABLE VEGETABLE SAUTE~

This dish does not require any salt or spices because the ingredients, if fresh, give it so much taste. It also looks beautiful. A great dish for warm weather, does not need reheating, and will taste great at room temperature the next day.

2 cups of chickpeas
1 medium head of cauliflower, cut into flowerets
1 ripe mango, peeled and cut into chunks
1 red pepper, cut into chunks
1 cup yellow raisins
oil for skillet

Steam cauliflower flowerets al dente

Heat oil in skillet until reasonably hot
Place chickpeas, mango, red pepper chunks and raisins in hot skillet, mix and cook until red pepper and mango soften.

Add cauliflower, mix well and heat

Serve over rice

Serves 6

Variations: Add 1 cup of green beans cut into inch pieces, or
1 cup of blanched almonds, or
1 cup of fresh pineapple chunks, or all three

Tip: If you continue to add ingredients, you will be able to serve up to 10

~SPINACH SPANATIKA~

This is a vegan version of an old favorite, and very easy to make. It goes well with many other old favorites, such as baked potatoes, salad, or corn bread, and tastes good served at room temperature the next day. Varieties of vegan cream cheese and tofu sour cream can be found in local supermarkets. You might want to try one or two brands to decide which one you like---and check the sugar content.

Heat oven 350°

> 1 pound of spinach, washed and shredded
> 1 Tablespoon olive oil
> 1 package of "Better than Cream Cheese Cream Cheese"
> 1 container of tofu sour cream
> 1/2 cup wheat germ
> 2 Tablespoons oregano.
> 2-3 Tablespoons vegan parmesan cheese
> 2-3 Tablespoons paprika

Oil an oven 9 X 11 Pyrex casserole

Mix the first five ingredients well
Sprinkle vegan parmesan cheese over the top, then sprinkle the paprika

Bake for 40 minutes, or until top is browned.

Serves 8

Note: Use the French Onion "Better than Cream Cheese Cream Cheese" for a peppier taste.

~WHITE BEAN STEW WITH CARAMELIZED ONIONS~

This recipe has the advantage that the dish can be served hot or cold; can be prepared a day in advance. Leftovers will do well the next day.

2 Tablespoons olive oil
2 medium onions, thinly sliced into rounds
1 Tablespoon brown sugar, packed
2-1/2 Tablespoons balsamic vinegar
2 15.5-ounce cans cannelloni beans, drained
1 Tablespoon dried rosemary
1/2 cup dry white wine
1 teaspoon salt, or to taste
freshly ground pepper to taste

Heat olive oil in medium size pan over high heat.

Add onions, cover, reduce heat to low, cook onions about 30-45 minutes, stirring occasionally, until soft and golden in color.

Sprinkle the brown sugar and balsamic vinegar over onions, cook for one minute.

Add the beans, crush the rosemary over the beans.

Add remaining ingredients. When mixture comes to a boil, reduce heat to low, simmer uncovered for 5 minutes.

Serves 5-6

~WHITE BEAN STEW WITHOUT CARAMELIZED ONIONS~

The stew should be thick, but not dry. For the waist-conscious cook, this recipe has no added fat, yet is very creamy.

> 1 and 1//2 cups small white beans
> 1 and 1/2 inch piece kombu
> 2 bay leaves
> 2 small Yukon Gold potatoes
> 1 large carrot
> 1/2 cup thinly sliced burdock root
> 1 teaspoon vegan Worcestershire sauce
> 1 teaspoon Herbamaire ®

Rinse the beans and soak in water for at least four hours or overnight.

Discard soaking water.

Fill a 1-1/2 quart pot about 3/4 full, bring to a simmer, add the beans, bay leaf and the kombu cut in small pieces with a scissors.

Check the beans frequently, stirring fairly often. When almost done, add potatoes diced small and the sliced carrot and burdock. (Never add salt or tomato products to beans until they are soft or they may stay hard).

When the beans are done add the Herbamaire® and the Worcestershire sauce, stir and simmer a few more minutes.

Serves 5-6

Note: Burdock root is found in the produce section of health food stores. It is excellent for winter cooking because it is strengthening.

~BAKED BEANS WITH APPLE AND ONION CASSEROLE~

This combination of green apple and onion gives a new twirl to an old idea, and it's easy to make. Combine with seitan slices or tofu squares for a hearty casserole on a winter night. Best when eaten the same day it is made.

Preparation: Half a package of baked beans, soaked, and cooked 2-3 hours until soft
Heat oven to 350°

1 middle sized onion
1 large green apple
1 cup of vegan cheddar cheese
1/2 teaspoon cayenne pepper

Pureé beans in food processor. Chop onion in food processor

Chop apple, but not too fine. Leave it chunky, or you will get apple juice

Grate vegan cheese in food processor or with a cheese grater.

Mix ingredients together.

Lightly oil 6 X 4 loaf pan, put mixture in and bake for 20 minutes.

Turn off the oven. Cover with barbecued seitan steaks or tofu squares after the casserole is cooked. Keep warm in the oven until ready to serve.

Serves 6

~MULTI-NATIONAL POTATO CASSEROLE~

In this age of global trotting and international sensitivities, the following recipe is one that can be served to anyone from any country. An Iranian-born Jewish woman of Kurdish-Iraqi descent taught the original version of this dish to her Ashkenazic daughter-in-law from Chelsea, MA., who changed it to suit her cooking style. (The original version was made in individual deep-fried portions.) We adapted it further for the vegan kitchen, because it is, in its way, a microcosm of Jewish culinary history. This dish is also appropriate for Purim, and doubly appropriate for a Purim Shabbat, and it tastes just as good at room temperature the next day.

Preheat oven to 375°.

2 Tablespoons oil
4 cups sliced mushrooms (about 1 pound)
2 cups chopped onions
1/2 cup slivered almonds
1/2 cup golden raisins
Salt and pepper
8 medium redskin potatoes, boiled and peeled
2 teaspoons ground cumin
1/2 teaspoon ground turmeric
1-3 Tablespoons warm water, stock,
      or reserved potato cooking water
2 Tablespoons margarine, melted

Heat 2 Tablespoons oil in 10 " or 12" skillet.
Sauté onions and mushrooms until onions are tender and mushrooms give up their liquid. (You may need to cover the skillet for part of the cooking time, especially if you are using a 10" skillet.) Add raisins, almonds, and a sprinkling of salt.

Oil an 8 cup casserole, about 7" x 11", or 8" x 8"
(*Continue*)

Mash potatoes, adding 1 Tablespoon or more of warm liquid if necessary to make the potatoes workable. Season with cumin, turmeric, salt and pepper, and add most of the melted margarine.

Place a layer of mashed potatoes in the bottom of casserole. Cover it with mushroom mixture.

Top with the rest of the potatoes, and brush with remaining margarine.

Bake for about 40 minutes.

Serves 8.

Variation: If you do not want to use cumin, flavor potatoes with a small chopped onion sautéed in melted margarine or oil. but use turmeric for its rich golden color.

Tip: Add shredded sautéed tofu on top, or a side dish of sautéed tofu triangles for protein.

~~~~~~~~~~~~~~~~~~~~~~~~~~~~~

Friday is always a hectic day. I think any Jewish house-wife will tell you that. First you have to look good. Then you have to have the house look good, and have the table look good, and have the food look good. On Friday I have the first morning appointment at the hairdresser.
Sandy Goodglick, in Dr. Ron Wolfson, Shabbat:
The Family Guide to Preparing for and Celebrating the Sabbath.

~TEMPEH TUNA~

This dish is made in two steps, with two lists of ingredients. Great to serve for a summer meal and have enough left over for the next day to eat as sandwiches. For an interesting presentation, serve rolled up in a tortilla or any type of soft roll. Particularly good for an intimate Friday night Shabbat dinner.

Preheat oven to 350°.

Step one:
> 1 pound package tempeh
> 3 cups water

Cut tempeh into cubes, bring water to a boil and add tempeh. Cook 5 minutes on a medium boil then drain.

> Olive oil
> 2 Tablespoons tamari
> 2 Tablespoons water
> 1 Tablespoon oil
> 1 Tablespoon maple syrup

Spray or brush a baking sheet with oil. Toss tempeh with the oil, tamari and maple syrup. Spread out on a baking sheet and bake 20 to 25 minutes stirring frequently until brown. Remove from oven and cool.

Step two: Mash with fork and combine with the following 8 ingredients.

> 3 Tablespoons organic sweet pickle relish (optional)
> 1 Tablespoon Dijon mustard
> 3/4 cup egg free mayonnaise (Nayonaise or Veganaise)
> 1 red onion, diced small
> 2 stalks celery, diced small
> 1 carrot, grated
> 1 Tablespoon fresh dill weed, minced or 1 teaspoon dried dill
> Freshly ground black pepper

Serves 4

~TEMPEH TUNA-LIKE~

Here is a one-step simpler approach to the same dish. This will not taste like tuna, but it has the same satisfaction and texture, and you will enjoy it for a light summer Shabbat and for a Shabbat lunch. It works well in lettuce cups or on crackers. great for a warm weather meal. and it can be made early in the day.

I eight ounce package tempeh (garden vegetable variety is good for this)
1 Tablespoon olive oil
1 Tablespoon maple syrup
2 Tablespoons tamari or Braggs Liquid
1 small red onion
2 stalks celery
1 large carrot
1 Tablespoon fresh dill or 1 teaspoon dried
1/2 cup vegan mayonnaise (grape seed variety)
1 heaping teaspoon brown mustard
3 Tablespoons sweet pickle relish
1/8 teaspoon turmeric
A few grindings of black pepper

In a skillet large enough to hold the tempeh bring a cup of water to boil, add the tempeh and simmer on each side for 2-3 minutes.
Empty the water, pat the tempeh dry. Rinse the skillet, add the oil, maple syrup and the tamari or Braggs.
Cut the tempeh into very fine dice and sauté lightly while preparing the vegetables. Tempeh should be brown, but not too dark. Stir often.
Dice the onion, celery and carrot fine or put them in the food processor for about 12 pulses. (Don't let it get mushy.) Put the tempeh cubes in a fairly large bowl, allow to cool, add the diced vegetables, stir together,
Snip the fresh dill with a scissors and add, or add the dried dill. Add the rest of the ingredients and mix well, break the cubes a bit smaller, but don't mash.

Serves 5-6.
Note: Buy organic pickle relish, as well as ketchup and mustard, to avoid high fructose corn syrup in these products.

~SZECHWAN SEITAN~

A basic dish to serve with noodles, rice, or any other carb. But if you are allergic to gluten, seitan is not for you. It is the gluten that makes seitan possible and gives it that sticky elastic texture. Brown rice and other gluten-free flours are tricky to bake with because they lack gluten, which is why gluten-free baked goods are often marginal, although there have been valiant attempts to make a gluten-free seitan.
Preheat oven to 375 °.

Step one

Spray of olive oil
1 pound seitan
1 Tablespoon peanut oil
2 Tablespoons tamari
1/4 cup water
1 Tablespoon maple syrup

Spray or brush a baking pan with oil. Slice the seitan into strips and whisk together the rest of the ingredients. Pour over the seitan, combining well and spread on the baking sheet. Bake, stirring frequently until seitan is very brown and caramelized, about 30 to 35 minutes.

Step two

1 Tablespoon toasted sesame oil
1 medium onion, sliced thin
3 cloves garlic, sliced
1 Tablespoon fresh grated ginger or
1 teaspoon ground
2 carrots, cut into thin strips
2 celery stalks, sliced thin
1 red bell pepper, sliced into thin strips
1/8 teaspoon red pepper flakes
1/2 teaspoon salt
1/2 cup water
2 Tablespoons tamari soy sauce
1 Tablespoon rice or maple syrup
1 Tablespoon rice vinegar

(Continue)

1 1/2 Tablespoons arrowroot
1/4 cup water
2 scallions chopped
Toasted Sesame seeds, optional

Warm oil in skillet and heat on medium. Add onion and sauté for 1 minute.
Stir in garlic and ginger and cook another minute.
Toss in carrots, celery and bell pepper, sprinkle with cayenne and salt.
Sauté until vegetables are tender but crisp and bright, about 5 minutes.
Pour in water, soy sauce, syrup and vinegar and bring to a low boil.
Dissolve arrowroot in the water to make a thin paste, pour into skillet and stir until thickened and clear.
Add seitan, thoroughly combine and garnish with scallions and sesame seeds.

Serves 6.

Note: This dish goes well over almost any carb, especially rice or millet

~~~~~~~~~~~~~~~~~~~~~~~~~~~~~~~~~~

A Jewish home is a place where you say mazel tov if some-one breaks a plate instead of pretending not to notice. A place where husbands help--on good ancient rabbinic insistence--in the preparations. Where the Kiddush wine-- that perverse mixture of port and cough syrup--still tastes better than the discreetly supervised Chateau Bois de Saint-Jean.

Rabbi Jonathan Sacks,
"The Home Where Warmth Rules Over Technology."

~FOUR-CAN TVP CHILI~

From Kara Willliam Wortman, who combines a career in law with gourmet cooking, which goes to show that any good ingredients--or talents-- can mix.

Chilis are great for Shabbat meals because they can serve many, and taste just as good the next day at room temperature. Best to use for winter Shabbats, if you intend to use leftovers, because beans can't be trusted to stay too long in the warm weather.

This dish is surprisingly light, though it looks heavy, when done. Like Vietnamese meals, this chile/stew is the main dish. Wonderful for a large Shabbat crowd. Serve in soup bowls with large slices of challah. Guests will want to mop up the bowl with the challah slices. Goes well with a salad of mixed greens or cucumber salad or cucumber and radish salad.

2 cups textured vegetarian protein (TVP)
2 cups boiling water
2-4 Tablespoons olive oil
1 large green pepper, seeded and chopped
3 large onions, coarsely chopped
3-5 cloves garlic, minced
2 Tablespoons vinegar
1 Tablespoon cumin
1 Tablespoon cocoa powder
3-5 Tablespoons chili powder
Salt
Black pepper
Dash cayenne pepper
1 15.25-ounce can of corn, drained
1 40.5--ounce kidney beans, drained
1 28-ounce can tomatoes, juice included
1 6-ounce can tomato paste
3/4 cup water

(Continue)

Place the TVP in a medium bowl. Pour two cups boiling water over the TVP. Let sit for 10 minutes until water is absorbed.

Heat oil in a large pot over medium heat. Add the green pepper, onions, and garlic.

Cook, stirring frequently until vegetables are soft and translucent.

Add TVP vinegar, cumin, cocoa powder, chili powder, salt, pepper, cayenne and stir well.

Add the corn, beans, tomatoes and tomato paste. Use a wooden spoon to break the tomatoes into large pieces. Add 3/4 cup water and mix well.

Bring chili to a boil, reduce heat, simmer for at least 20 minutes. Adjust seasonings.

Serves 10 hearty bowls

~~~~~~~~~~~~~~~~~~~

Our lives, our Shabbatot have changed. And as I sit at the head of our table, I think of the women throughout Jewish history who have presided at Shabbat tables by default or by design, women who have guided children as contentious as mine into a Shabbat of nourishing food and healing song. I think of the many women who juggle their passion for teaching Judaism with their love for their families.

Sue Levi Elwell, "A Family Shabbat: Dreams and Reality"

~EGGPLANT STEAKS SMOTHERED UNDER VEGETABLES~

These can be served at room temperature the next day and are particularly good served in sandwiches. But served on a lettuce leaf, make a pretty presentation.

Heat over 375 °

Oil for cookie tray
1 large eggplant, wash skin, do not peel
3 carrots, chopped
3 ribs of celery, chopped
4 large mushrooms, sliced
2 Tablespoons parsely
Garlic powder
Basil and/or oregano

Slice eggplant into 1/2 inch slices.

Oil cookie tray and place the eggplant slices on the tray.
Sprinkle each slice with garlic powder and/or oregano or basil leaves.
Bake for 20 minutes. Turn over, bake another 15-20 minutes until soft, but not mushy.

In the meantime, oil skillet and sauté chopped carrots and celery for about 10 minutes. Add water if necessary to keep vegetables moist.

Add sliced mushrooms and continue to sauté until vegetables are done. Mix together. Place a generous heap on each eggplant slice, and serve.

Serves 6-8

~VEGETABLE NUT LOAF I~

This dish was adapted from Rose Friedman's *Jewish Vegetarian Cooking*, one of the very first Jewish vegetarian cookbooks. It can be prepared early in the day and popped into the oven in late afternoon. The trick to this loaf is to baste it often and keep it moist. Use whatever nuts you prefer except peanuts, and do not use salted nuts. A variety of almonds, walnuts, and cashews is best. In order to keep the expense of this dish down, buy nuts on sale in advance or in bulk and freeze them for later use, which is a good idea to do in general. Nuts keep well in the freezer. This loaf is also fabulous served at room temperature the next day.

Preheat oven to 350°.

> 1 large onion, finely chopped
> 3 cloves of garlic, finely chopped
> 2 large carrots, grated
> 3 cups of mixed ground nuts
> 1 cup matzo meal
> 4 Tablespoons tomato paste
> 1 large onion, sliced thinly
> 2-1/2 cups vegetable stock

Mix all ingredients well, except vegetable stock and sliced onion.
Grease ovenproof casserole; place sliced onions all over the bottom.
Form nut and carrot mixture into a loaf and place on top of sliced onions.

Bake 45 minutes. Baste with vegetable stock every 20 minutes.
Remove from oven and let cool for ten-fifteen minutes.

Serves 8

Tips: Ingredients can be cut in half for a smaller loaf, but it is very good the next day if left at room temperature; so don't worry about having too much. When you have the oven going, bake herbed oven roasted potatoes.

~VEGETABLE NUT LOAF ll~

This dish is originally from Freya Dinsha's recipe in her book, *The Vegan Kitchen,* and we reproduced it in *The Vegetarian Pesach Cookbook.* It's a classic and deserves another mention, because it does not require much cooking in the oven since the ingredients are precooked and, like many vegetarian loafs, will keep well for the next day. This loaf, like the previous one, is made with matzoh meal and can be made for a Passover Shabbat.
Preheat oven to 350 °

Oil for oven dish
2/3 cups of Brazil nuts
2/3 cups of filberts
2 medium potatoes, peeled
2 small zucchini squash
1 medium sweet potato
            (or small butternut squash)
1 large carrot
4 ribs celery
1 small onion
2-2/3 cups matzoh meal
1-1/2 teaspoons mixed herbs
4 teaspoons olive oil
2 Tablespoons paprika

Cover nuts with water and simmer about 1 hour until soft
Drain, dry, and grind
Dice all the vegetables and cook together in 3-1/2 cups water for 30 minutes.
Drain and mash vegetables. Mix in the nuts
Add the matzoh meal, oil, and herbs. Mix well.
Put mixture into a small oiled baking pan, press down well. Sprinkle paprika evenly over the top.
Bake for 10 minutes. Imagine! Only ten minutes.

Serves 4-6
Variation: For a richer taste, cover loaf with a mushroom sauce, or with cooked mushrooms and/or caramelized onions.

~MEATLESS LOAF~

This dish takes time but is excellent for a Shabbat dinner because it can feed many people, keeps well and can be served chilled or at room temperature the next day. It also makes a wonderful deli dish for Saturday lunch, served in sandwiches with a good mustard, horseradish, or vegenaise condiment.

Preheat oven to 375 °.

2 Tablespoons olive oil
1 large onion, diced
1 cup chopped walnuts
1 cup rolled oats (not instant variety)
1/2 pound mushrooms, sliced
2 cups vegetable broth
(vegetable cubes can be used to make broth)
2 cloves garlic, minced
1 cup grated carrot
3 Tablespoons Dijon, or other hearty mustard
4 Tablespoons tomato sauce
2 Tablespoons soy or tamari sauce
1 pound firm tofu, drained
2 Tablespoons arrowroot powder
2 cups whole wheat bread crumbs,
or other preferred bread crumbs

In a large skillet, heat 1 Tablespoon oil. Sauté onion until partly caramelized, about 20 minutes. Stir occasionally. Transfer onions to a large mixing bowl.
In the same skillet, heat remaining oil, add walnuts, and sauté over medium heat 3 minutes. Add oats, sauté another 3 minutes, stirring. Add mushrooms, broth, and garlic. Reduce heat to low. Cook until mushrooms soften and stock is absorbed, about 8 minutes.
While oat mixture cooks, add carrot, mustard, tomato paste or sauce, soy sauce or tamari. Add oat mixture to bowl with onions, and set aside.
Purée tofu and arrowroot powder in blender or food processor until smooth. Add to oat-carrot mixture, and mix well.
Add bread crumbs and mix again. Pour into large oiled loaf pan. Bake 40-50 minutes. Cool 30 minutes before slicing.
Serves 8-10 and more depending on side dishes

אהבה

Ahavah
Love

There is an unmistakable sexual charge to Friday evening, shaped in part by the recognition that after services the two main things that are on the religious agenda are a delicious meal and sex. It's wonderful to allow these anticipations to mix with the sensuous religious texts and to savor in anticipation a coming sensual delight. Far from demeaning spirituality, sex and food are critical elements of a Jewish spirituality. Pleasure is good **Michael Lerner, Shabbat**

~STUFFED CABBAGE WITH KASHA~

A traditional dish that we can't pass up, one that has several variations, and you can make up your own as well.

There are many ways to peel off the large leaves from cabbage to use. (See instructions for *Stuffed Cabbage with Butternut Squash*) The following is recommended if you have the time: Freeze the cabbage head for two days, thaw it overnight in a colander in the sink; the leaves will be pliable and come apart easily. Otherwise, bring a large pot of water to boil and cook the cabbage for about 5 minutes to soften the leaves (as in *Cabbage With Butternut Squash*) Drain and set aside in the colander.

The tomato sauce recommended below may seem fussy, but it is so good, it's worth learning and trying it with other recipes.

Preheat oven to 350 °.

> 1 large head cabbage, about 3 pounds
> 1/4 cup oil
> 1 medium onion, finely chopped
> 2 cups kasha
> Salt and freshly ground pepper to taste
> 4 cups water
> recipe tomato sauce (see below)

Sauté the onion in the oil in a heavy 2 or 3 quart pot.
Add the kasha, and turn it in the oil to coat all grains.
Add salt, pepper and water. Bring to a boil, reduce heat, and simmer, covered, about 15 or 20 minutes. Check at 15 minutes.
Remove from heat when just a small amount of water remains in the bottom of the pot. Let sit a few minutes until the kasha absorbs the water. Stir to fluff and separate the grains.

Separate the cabbage leaves. On each leaf, place 2 or 3 heaping tablespoons of kasha. Fold one edge of the leaf over the filling, tuck in the sides, and roll.
Cut up any leftover cabbage, and place in an oiled baking dish or casserole. Place rolls seam side down on top. Pour in tomato sauce almost to cover.
(Continue)

~65~

Sauce

1 28 ounce can + 1 16 ounce can tomatoes
9 ounces tomato paste (1 1/2 6 ounce cans)
6 Tablespoons brown sugar
6 Tablespoons vinegar
Rind of 1 1/2 oranges, grated
1 teaspoon salt, or to taste
1 1/2 teaspoons basil
Freshly ground black pepper to taste

Drain some liquid from the tomatoes into a heavy 3 quart pot.
Stir in the tomato paste until smooth. Add remaining contents of tomato cans.
Mash the tomatoes with a potato masher to break them up.
Stir in the rest of the ingredients.
Simmer about 10 minutes. Stir and add to baking pan. Cover with foil or lid and
bake about 2 hours or until cabbage is tender.
Uncover for the last 45 minutes to allow the sauce to thicken. Baste occasionally.
Taste, and add more sugar or vinegar if necessary.

Serves 8-10.

The table was well spread with all manner of fruit, beans,
green stuffs and good pies, plum water tasting like wine.

S. Y. Agnon, *The Bridal Canopy*

~STUFFED CABBAGE WITH SQUASH~

Squash makes a great stuffing for many traditional dishes, such as ravioli, and this is one more tasty variation on the traditional cabbage stuffed with meat. It is succulent, excellent for a large company Shabbat, and keeps well for the next day

Preheat oven to 350 °.

One large head of green cabbage, washed
4-5 cups of mashed butternut squash
Oil for a 9 X 12 baking dish with cover
1 large cup of walnuts, chopped
2 teaspoons nutmeg
Pinch of salt

Sauce

One 16 ounce can of tomato sauce
3 Tablespoons mild vinegar, or to taste
1-1/2 Tablespoons ground cinnamon
1 cup raisins (optional)

Bake squash until soft. In the meantime, boil water in a very large pot. Immerse the whole head of cabbage into the boiling water, and boil for about 20 minutes or until the outer leaves of the cabbage are limp. Drain the cabbage, set aside and cool.

Remove squash from oven when it is done, cut in half, clean out the seeds and pulp, and mash the squash. Do not mash in a food processor. You don't want this too fine.

Add the chopped walnuts and cinnamon to the squash.

When cabbage is cool enough to handle, gently pull away the large outer leaves, place a large Tablespoon of squash in each leaf, roll up, pin sides together, and place in baking dish.

Mix the ingredients for the sauce and pour over the stuffed cabbage. Bake for 20 minutes. Remove, cover dish to prevent the sauce from drying out.

Serves 10

~SWEET AND SOUR CAULIFLOWER BAKE~

This dish looks beautiful and tastes like it looks. Serve surrounded by cherry tomatoes.

Preheat oven to 375 °.

>1 Tablespoon oil
>1 medium onion
>1 large head cauliflower
>3 medium sweet potatoes
>3 Macintosh apples

Sauce

>1 8 ounce can tomato sauce
>2 Tablespoons tomato paste
>1 Tablespoon plus 1 teaspoon balsamic vinegar
>2 Tablespoons cinnamon

Oil a 9 X 12 baking or Pyrex dish
Slice onions and layer the bottom of the dish
Wash cauliflower, break into small flowerets, and place on top of the onions
Wash and cut the potatoes and apples into chunks and place on top of the cauliflower

Blend all the ingredients for sauce and pour over the dish, coating the vegetables and the fruit thoroughly.

Bake 1 hour in oiled baking dish with cover.

Serves 6
Variation: Add 1 cup of apricots or one cup of diced dates--or both

Tip: To increase servings, add one more sweet potato and one more apple, and oil a larger baking dish. Can be served with rice, and will then serve 8-9 without adding the extra potato and apple.

~EASY CAULIFLOWER PIE~

Will keep well at room temperature for Shabbat lunch, so double the ingredients and make two, and have a company dish for the next day. Don't forget to bake some sweet potatoes to go along with this pie.

Preheat oven 375 °

1 pie crust of your choosing
1 large head of cauliflower
3 large scallions, chopped fine
Pinch of salt
2 Tablespoons paprika

Separate flowerets and steam until just soft
Mix in scallions and salt, pile into pie crust, top with generous sprinkling of paprika,

Bake 25-30 minutes

Serves 8

Variations: Make pie crust from 1-1/2 cups chopped unsalted mixture of almonds, cashews or brazil nuts, mixed with 2 Tablespoons margarine to soften

If using plain pie crust, mix 1/2 cup of vegan parmesan cheese into the flowerets and sprinkle 1/2 cup of vegan parmesan cheese with paprika on top of pie.

~MANICOTTI BAKE WITH SLOPPY JOE~

An old favorite, everyone knows it. This one is for vegan lovers of manicotti. Though traditionally served hot, it will taste well at room temperature.

Preheat oven 350°

> Oil
> 1 package of firm tofu
> 1 medium size onion, chopped
> 1/2 large green pepper, cut in small pieces
> 1/2 cup black olives
> 1 eight ounce can tomato sauce--or your favorite
> pasta topping (see the other tomato sauces)
> 1/2 cup vegan parmesan cheese, or nutritional
> yeast or 3-4 slices vegan white cheddar

Boil water in a large pot for the manicotti, cook until al dente, drain

Oil a large skillet
Sauté chopped onions about 3-5 minutes
Add green pepper pieces
Add tofu, mashed up in skillet, add olives, mix well
Add tomato sauce, simmer about five minutes

Oil a large lasagna pan with cover
Stuff the manicotti with the sloppy joe sauce and place in oiled pan
Sprinkle cheese or layer down a top layer of cheese slices, cover with more
tomato sauce (don't drench it), cover with aluminum foil and bake 20 min-
utes
Goes well with green salad

Serves 8

~FETTUCINI ALFONSO~

Noodle dishes always go a long way and can be served at room temperature the next day. Though dairy free, the sauce on this noodle dish is rich and sumptuous.

1/2 pound of egg-free fetuccini noodles
2 teaspoons olive oil
1 medium size onion, cut in large dice
4 cloves of garlic, chopped
1/2 cup water
2 teaspoons yellow mustard
1/2 cup toasted pine nuts
2 teaspoons soy sauce or Braggs Liquid
2 teaspoons mild chile powder
1 cup nutritional yeast
1/2 teaspoon salt
A few grindings black pepper

Chop the onion and garlic. Put up the pot of water to cook the fettucini. While it is coming to a boil, lightly toast the pine nuts in a heavy skillet, stirring frequently. Watch carefully or they will start to burn.

Sauté the onion and garlic in the oil until soft. Put all ingredients in the food processor and process until mostly smooth yet still a bit grainy. The pasta can cook while you are doing this.

Drain noodles and serve with the sauce over it. If the Alfonso is a bit too thick, thin with a bit of the pasta water.

Serves 6

~TRANSYLVANIAN GOULASH~

Like so many recipes that originally had meat in them, this Transylvanian goulash proves that vegetarian versions are every bit as tasty as the other kind. This one comes from The Mid-Hudson Vegetarian Society, and when Robbie Schiff says of the paprika "use only this kind," she means "use only this kind." But you can cheat, and the dish will still be great.

1 - 28 oz. Jar sauerkraut
1 medium cabbage, sliced, use all but the core
5 or 6 medium fresh tomatoes
1 15 oz. can diced tomatoes (or in winter use 2 cans of tomatoes instead)
1 medium to large onion, diced
2 Tablespoons sweet Hungarian paprika (use only this kind)
2 Tablespoons caraway seeds
2 cloves garlic
2-3 Tablespoons olive oil
Juice of 1 lemon
2 bay leaves

Sauté the onion and garlic in the olive oil until it gently turns color, transfer to a large pot, add the sauerkraut, paprika, mix together, then add the rest of the ingredients, stir well and let simmer about an hour until the flavors blend well. After it has been simmering about 15 minutes, taste and add more paprika, as needed.

Rinse two cups of long grain brown rice, (jasmine is nice, but any kind of brown rice will do.) Bring three cups of water to a boil, add 1 teaspoon sea salt, then the rice, stir until the water returns to a boil, then cover and simmer for 35 minutes. The heavier the pot the better the rice will cook. A flame deflector under the pot is good for cooking grain. After 35 minutes, turn off the flame and wait another 10 minutes to open the lid and stir.

To serve, put some rice on a plate or in a bowl, and ladle the goulash over it.

Serves 10

~ CROCKPOT GOULASH~

Great for the cook with more time in the morning than in the evening when she comes home from work. When she opens the door the odor from this dish will invade her kitchen and make it smell like the Shabbat kitchen you remember when your Bubbee made Shabbat. Robin Robertson suggests a 4 quart cooker for the following recipe, but it can be made in a 6 quart cooker. Adding four or five large carrots, quartered, will add volume to the crock pot and color to the dish.

2 Tablespoons olive oil
1 pound tempeh, cut into 1/2 inch slices
1 small yellow onion, halved and thinly sliced
2 cups sauerkraut, drained and rinsed
One 14.5 ounce can of diced tomatoes, drained
1 Tablespoon sweet Hungarian pepper
1/4 cup dry white wine
1 teaspoon caraway seeds (optional)
2 Tablespoons tomato paste
4 or 5 large carrots, quartered
1 1/2 cup vegetable stock
salt and freshly ground pepper to taste
1/2 cup tofu sour cream

Heat 1 Tablespoon of oil in a large skillet over medium heat. Add tempeh, brown for about ten minutes. Remove to another dish and set aside.
Do not clean skillet. Add remaining Tablespoon of oil over medium heat, add the sliced onion, cover and cook about five minutes, until softened.

Transfer onions to crockpot. Add the tempeh and the rest of the ingredients, except the tofu sour cream.
Cover and cook on low for 6 hours.

Just before serving, drain off about 1/2 cup of liquid from the crockpot, mix with tofu sour cream, whisk together. Stir liquid back into the goulash and serve over rice or noodles that are ready.

Serves 6

~VEGAN LASAGNA~

Easy to make, this recipe has the same richness as lasagna made with cheese, but is 100% animal free and 0% cholesterol! Serve with leafy greens like sautéed collard greens. Use whatever organic veggies your farmers' market or health food store has that are freshest. Add garlic bread or toasted challah and you're celebrating Shabbat in Rome.

Preheat oven to 350 F°

8 oz box whole-wheat lasagna
1 pound firm tofu
Italian seasonings, oregano, thyme, basil
Lemon juice
Vegetarian Worcestershire sauce
        (The Wizard's brand is tasty)
3 or 4 large Portobello mushrooms
Olive oil
1 medium eggplant
1 25 oz jar pasta sauce
2 large onions
4 cloves garlic
nutritional yeast
9 x 13 oblong pan

Peel the eggplant. Slice and sprinkle with sea salt, and let sit while you do the rest. This will draw out any bitterness.

Dice the onion and garlic and sauté in olive oil slowly until onions become golden. Set aside. While the onions are cooking, bring water to boil and cook the noodles according to package directions.
Drain the tofu. Press with a heavy plate on top to remove more water. As you do the other things, check and press the plate down a few times to get out additional water.

(Continue)

Slice the mushrooms and sauté in a little olive oil with the Worcestershire sauce (about two Tablespoons). Add some water and a bit of leftover wine (if you have some around). When the mushrooms are almost done, add one third of the onion garlic mixture, stir together, turn off heat.

Lightly oil the glass pan. Place a layer of cooked noodles in pan. Spread the mushroom mixture over the noodles, add the sauce.

Dice or crumble the tofu (large crumbles) and sauté in a bit of oil, add some lemon juice and the Italian seasonings to taste. Add some of the onions and garlic. Sauté until lightly browned. Put another layer of noodles in the pan; add tofu, then more sauce.

Wash the salt off the eggplant slices, and dice fairly small. Sauté in oil, use more oil than you did for the mushrooms or tofu. Season eggplant according to taste. Add the rest of the onion garlic mixture.

Add another layer of noodles, then the eggplant, more sauce. Then put another layer of noodles (you are almost done) the rest of the sauce and some nutritional yeast (about a third of a cup) if desired.

Cover with foil or a cookie sheet and bake for about 45 minutes.

Serves 6 - 8 generous portions

~~~~~~~~~~~~~~~~~~~~~~~~~~~~~

You shall proclaim the Shabbat an oneg--
 a delight
says the prophet (Isaiah 58:13),

What constitutes a delight?

One should prepare the most delicious foods
And drinks for one's Shabbat meals.

Rambam, Laws of Shabbat, chapter 30: 1, 7.

~INDIAN INSPIRED SKILLET DISH FOR TWO~

We went to the International Vegetarian Conference in Goa, India in October 2006, and then spent 10 days traveling in India. The variety of curries in India are of course spectacular. We visited a spice plantation and regret that we didn't bring back pounds of saffron, which is the world's most expensive spice and grows abundantly in India. Columbus knew what he was doing when he went in search of the fabulous spices that come from India. But in deference to the taste buds and pocketbooks of most cooks, the following recipe does not contain saffron and the spices are mild, but you can always increase them to suit your taste.

1-1/2 Tablespoons oil
1 medium red onion
one half pound firm tofu
1 large Yukon gold potato
1 broccoli stalk of flowerets
2 carrots
(all the above diced)

1 teaspoon turmeric
1 teaspoon sweet red Hungarian paprika
1/4 teaspoon each dry mustard and ginger
I Tablespoon vegetarian Worcestershire sauce
Sea salt and ground black pepper to taste

Sauté the onion in a heavy skillet in 1/2 Tablespoon oil and small amount of water. When onions are almost soft add tofu, potato, broccoli and carrot, sauté, stir often, adding small amounts of water to brown the food without burning. After a minute or two, add the seasonings, then the rest of the oil, keep stirring until everything is done and slightly crispy. Serve over rice of your choice.

Serves two.
For 4 servings: Double the vegetables and the tofu. The spices are up to you. Will keep at room temperature for the next day, and flavor will increase.

Variation: Add a handful of yellow raisins in the final moments.

~SPANISH TEMPEH ROMESCO~

This dish is another two step recipe. Originally created by Pam Brown, who gives instructions for her recipes in this way. It seems sensible when dealing with a long list of ingredients. Start early and keep the dish in a warmer.
Preheat oven to 350 °

Step one

> Spray of olive oil
> 1 cup water
> 1 Tablespoon olive oil
> 2 Tablespoons tamari
> 1 lb. tempeh cut in 1-inch cubes
> 2 Tablespoons oil
> 1 slice whole-wheat bread, crust removed and diced
> 1 /2 cup almonds
> 1 large clove of garlic

Bring water, oil and tamari to a boil in a skillet. Add the tempeh. Cover and boil on medium heat until all the liquid has cooked away. Continue cooking the tempeh for a few more minutes until it browns.

In the meantime, warm a skillet, add the 2 Tablespoons oil. Toss in the bread and lightly brown.

Spread the almonds out in even layer on an unoiled baking sheet, place in oven and bake almonds for about 7 minutes until lightly brown. Cool and place the bread and almonds in a food processor or blender with the garlic and blend well.

Step two

> 1 red bell pepper, roasted and coarsely chopped
> 1/4 teaspoon red pepper flakes (optional)
> 2 Roma tomatoes, sliced in half and seeded
> 1/2 cup parsley leaves, coarsely chopped

(*Continue*)

1/2 teaspoon salt
1/2 teaspoon paprika
1 Tablespoon red wine vinegar
1 Tablespoon olive oil
1/2 cup water
Fresh ground pepper

To roast bell peppers, place under broiler and cook until skin is charred on all sides.

Put peppers in a bowl and cover with a plate for 10 minutes.

Discard seeds, peel off skin and pulp.

Add the bell pepper, pepper flakes, tomatoes, parsley, salt and paprika to the food processor and blend with the bread mixture until smooth.

With the motor running, pour in the wine vinegar, the olive oil and water. Taste for seasonings. Mix through tempeh, warm to serve.

Serves 4 to 6.

Note: This recipe will make extra sauce, which you can freeze and use over pasta, tofu or other grains in a future dish.

~~~~~~~~~~~~~~~~~~~~~~~~~~~~~~

The Talmud teaches:

As Shabbat drew near, the Sages
Would don their finest garments
And say to one another:

"Let us go out to greet the Sabbath Queen"
(Shabbat 119A)

~STIR FRIED GINGER CHINESE CABBAGE~
~WITH SAUTEED SEITAN~

Cabbage is a great health food, and this is an exotic way to cook it. Keep dish in a warmer until ready to serve.

2 teaspoons toasted sesame oil
1 teaspoon olive oil
1 medium onion, sliced thin
2 cloves garlic, diced
2 teaspoons freshly grated ginger or 1 teaspoon ground
    ginger
2 stalks celery, sliced thin
1 small red bell pepper, seeded with ribs removed and
sliced thin
2 carrots, sliced in thin strips
4 cups Chinese cabbage, sliced in thin strips (1 small
head)
1/2 teaspoon salt
1 Tablespoon tamari soy sauce
1 Tablespoon maple syrup
1 cup water
1 Tablespoon arrowroot flour
2 scallions, sliced thin

Heat a heavy skillet or a wok with the oils and add the onion. Sauté for 3 minutes, then add garlic and ginger, mix well. Cook another minute, then stir in the rest of the vegetables, one at a time.

Sprinkle with salt and cook on a medium high flame for 5 to 6 minutes or until the vegetables are tender, but crunchy. If the vegetables start to stick, add a few Table-spoons of water.
Combine all the above and add to the pan. Turn heat up to high and stir constantly until thickened. Garnish with the scallions. Serve with the seitan steaks.

Serves 6 to 8.

~BAKED OVEN TOFU FINGER STEAKS~

These tofu finger steaks keep well and taste equally good when served the next day at room temperature. If served the next day, place on a bed of lettuce and serve with a good mustard or a mild horse radish. This is easy to make and easy to eat. And since you're lighting the oven, why not serve with roasted root vegetables, like beets brushed with olive oil and oregano, or combine this dish with another oven baked dish, such as the roasted herb cauliflower. Great combination.

Preheat oven 400 $^\circ$

> 1 pound package of extra firm tofu
> 1/2 cup of Braggs or tamari or soy sauce
> 1 cup of whole wheat or soy flour
> 1/2 Tablespoon garlic powder
> 1/2 Tablespoon onion powder
> 1 Tablespoon crushed basil leaves
> 1/2 teaspoon sea salt
> 1-1/2 Tablespoons paprika

Drain tofu 1-2 hours in advance

Slice tofu lengthwise into one inch thick lengths

Marinate tofu sticks in sauce for about 1/2 hour

Oil a large cookie sheet, place tofu slices on cookie sheet, bake 20 minutes, turn over, bake another 10 minutes

Serves 4

TIP: To double and to have slices for the next day, double ingredients.

~BAKED SOUTHERN FRIED TOFU~

Like the previous recipe, easy to make and a nostalgia trip for those of us who miss the taste of fried foods. Yet the oil here is minimal---so not to worry.
Preheat oven to 425°

Step one

2 pounds extra firm tofu

1/4 cup tamari

1 Tablespoon water

1 teaspoon of olive oil

2 Tablespoons rice syrup or maple syrup

Cut tofu in half horizontally then cut across lengthwise into 4 pieces. You should have 8 slices of tofu. Whisk together the rest of the ingredients and pour over the tofu and marinate for 30 to 45 minutes or longer.

Step two

1/4 cup almonds

1 cup crackers, that have no or little salt

1 cup unbleached white flour

2 Tablespoons cornmeal or corn flour

1/2 teaspoon ground rosemary

1 teaspoon ground sage

1/2 teaspoon salt

1 teaspoon garlic granules

1 cup soy milk

Spray of olive oil

Grind almonds in food processor, then add crackers. Grind to a powder consistency. Mix with the flour, cornmeal, rosemary, sage, salt and garlic granules. Dip each piece of tofu in soy milk. Roll each stick in the crumb mixture coating thoroughly, then dip back into soy milk moistening well.
Spray each piece with oil and place on an oiled baking sheet and bake until brown, about 20 to 30 minutes. Turn over on the other side and bake another 10 minutes or until brown.

Serves 4 to 6.

~BARBECUED SEITAN~

In case you've been pining for the taste of barbecue something, here is a recipe to appease your longing. Worth making for the taste and because seitan is a good source of protein. Best served warm.

Preheat oven to 375 °

Step one

> 2 Tablespoons olive oil
> 1/4 cup Tamari sauce
> 1/4 cup maple syrup
> 2 pounds seitan, cut in chunks

Brush baking sheet with oil. Toss the tamari, oil, and syrup together with the seitan and spread on the baking sheet. Roast, stirring frequently until very brown, almost caramelized, about 25 minutes.

Step two

> Spray of oil
> 2 Tablespoons olive oil
> 1 large red bell pepper, diced in large pieces
> 1 large yellow bell pepper, diced in large pieces (if available)
> 1 large green bell peppers, diced in large pieces
> 1 large red onion, cut in thick slices
> 1/2 to 1 bottle of barbecue sauce

Spray or brush baking sheet with oil. Toss the first six ingredients of second group together and spread out on a baking sheet. Roast until tender, about 20 minutes.

Toss the seitan and vegetables together. Pour BBQ sauce over and stir until combined. Use 1/2 bottle for a milder taste or the whole bottle for a stronger BBQ flavor. Spread out in an even layer and roast another 5 or 6 minutes, or until brown almost caramelized. Serve over rice or pasta.

Serves 6 to 8

~LENTIL LOAF~

Another recipe that is packed with protein and taste. Add squash, sweet potatoes or oven-baked herbed potatoes. Great when chilled or served at room temperature.

Preheat oven to 350°

Olive oil
1 1/2 cups brown lentils, washed
6 cups water
1 bay leaf
2 cloves garlic, minced
1/2 teaspoon oregano
1/2 teaspoon thyme
1/2 cup bread or cracker crumbs
1 cup organic tomato sauce
2 Tablespoons vegetarian Worcestershire sauce (optional)
1 Tablespoon tamari
1 teaspoon olive oil
Salt and pepper to taste
Parsley

Oil a small size loaf pan. Bring water to a boil, add lentils and bay leaf and cook until very soft, about 25 to 30 minutes. Drain through a mesh strainer and remove the bay leaf. Stir the lentils and gently press with the back of a large spoon to remove any excess water. Pour lentils into a bowl and mash with a potato masher or large fork until they have the consistency of mashed potatoes.

Mix in the rest of the ingredients using only 1/4 cup of the ketchup. Season to your taste. Pack into the loaf pan, smoothing the top. Cover with foil and bake 35 minutes. Remove foil and cook another 15 minutes or until the sides are browned and the center is firm to the touch.

The last five minutes, spread the remaining 3/4 cup of ketchup over the loaf. Remove from oven and cool 30 minutes. Go around the edges with a knife to loosen. Gently tap out of pan on its side or invert on to a plate and then turn it over on to another plate so that the ketchup or sauce side is up. Garnish platter with parsley.

Serves 6-8

~CURRY MANGO BAKED TOFU~

An inspired fusion of protein, fruit and spice. You can substitute pineapple juice for the soy milk and use pineapple slices on the tofu instead of mango--or both for an Hawaiian fling.

Preheat oven to 400°

Spray of olive oil
2 1 lb. blocks extra firm tofu
2 Tablespoons tamari
3/4 cup water
1 teaspoon oil
2 ripe mangos and/or slices of pineapple
1/2 cup sweet white or mellow yellow miso
1-1/4 cup soy milk
1 teaspoon olive oil
1/4 cup brown rice syrup or maple syrup
1 teaspoon curry powder
1/2 teaspoon turmeric
1/2 teaspoon ground ginger
2 cloves garlic, minced
Small amount of oil in baking pan and spread with
  paper towel.

Spray a baking sheet with the oil. Arrange the tofu on the baking sheet and slice horizontally into 3 even pieces, then slice diagonally so that the tofu looks like a three cornered hat.

Mix the above ingredients together and pour over the tofu. Marinate for 10 minutes then bake in the oven for 20 minutes or until the tofu has browned.

Remove the tofu from the oven. Slice the mangos and/or pineapple into 12 thin slices. Blend the rest of the ingredients in the food processor or blender until creamy and pour over the tofu making sure each piece is covered. Arrange the mango slices on each piece and spray with a little oil. Return to oven and bake 20 more minutes or until the sauce has thickened and the tofu is browned.

Serves 6.

~LINGUINI WITH MOROCCAN LENTIL SAUCE~

You can prepare the lentils in advance and freeze them. In fact, since lentils are used so often in vegetarian dishes, you can prepare and freeze in 1/2 pound servings.

For an interesting presentation, this dish can be served in individual bowls

1 cup dry lentils, cooked
4 cups water
1 cinnamon stick
1 Tablespoon olive oil
1 cup yellow or white onions, diced
3 cloves garlic, minced
1 teaspoon finely grated ginger
2 teaspoons grated or finely minced lemon rind
2 carrots, diced small
2 stalks of celery, diced small
1-4.5 can diced tomatoes, drained, save liquid
2 Tablespoons tomato paste
1 teaspoon coriander
2 Tablespoons tamari
1/2 Tablespoon lemon juice
Salt and pepper, to taste

Wash lentils and add to pot with the water and cinnamon stick. Bring to a boil and cook for 30 minutes or until very soft. Remove cinnamon stick, drain lentils in a colander, setting the liquid aside.

Warm a skillet, add oil and stir in onions. Cook for a few minutes, toss in the garlic, ginger and lemon rind and sauté for 1 minute. Stir in the rest of the vegetables and cook on medium heat until tender, about 5 minutes.

Add lentils into the skillet and stir well. Mix in rest of the ingredients plus the drained tomato liquid and warm through about 5 to 7 minutes. If desired, mash the sauce with a potato masher or pulse quickly in the food processor for a creamier sauce, or serve as is.

(Continue)

1 lb. linguini
1 Tablespoon salt--or to taste
Olive oil
1/4 cup coarsely chopped almonds
Chopped parsley

Bring 4 quarts of water to a boil. Add salt and cook linguine according to the package directions. Drain, but do not rinse.

Toss with a little olive oil and place in a bowl or individual plates. Pour lentil sauce over individual servings of linguine. Garnish with chopped almonds and parsley.

Serves 6.

Note: For those who can take it, add 2 jalapenos seeded and chopped to sauce

~~~~~~~~~~~~~~~~~~~~~~~~~~~~~~~~~~~~~~

Among the Jews of Syria, the husband is responsible for doing all the shopping for Shabbat and for setting up the candlesticks for his wife to light. And many use twelve small hallah rolls for hamotzi, symbolic of the twelve shewbreads once used in the Temple.

Dr. Ron Wolfson, "The Family Guide to Preparing for and Celebrating the Sabbath," p.243.

~FETTUCCINI WITH MOCK ALFREDO SAUCE~

This is an old classic made over to suit the modern vegan taste. Best served warm.

2 teaspoons olive oil
3 cups mushrooms, sliced (button, porcini, portabella or any variety you like)
1 teaspoon tamari soy sauce

Clean mushrooms by wiping with a clean towel or quickly dunking them in a bowl of cold water, draining and patting dry with a paper towel.
Warm oil in a skillet. Add mushrooms and cook 5 minutes. Sprinkle tamari and continue sautéing mushrooms until they are browned and liquid has cooked away.

2 cloves garlic, minced
1/2 cup mellow miso
1/4 cup Earth Balance spread
1/2 cup tofu
1 Tablespoon Dijon mustard
2 Tablespoons olive oil
1 to 1 1/4 cup non dairy milk
1 Tablespoon lemon juice
1/2 cup parsley, washed and chopped fine

Add the garlic, miso, Earth Balance, tofu, mustard and oil to the food processor and blend until creamy, scraping down the bowl a few times. Slowly add milk and lemon juice until well blended. Sprinkle in 1/4 cup of the parsley and blend another minute.

1 Tablespoon salt
1 lb. fettuccine
1 Tablespoon olive oil
Parsley for garnish
Fresh ground pepper

(Continue)

Bring 4 quarts of water to a boil. Add salt and cook pasta al dente. While pasta is cooking, pour sauce into a small pot with very low heat, warm through, stirring constantly. If it is too thick, add a little water or non-dairy milk. Drain pasta. Do not rinse but toss with olive oil and mix thoroughly.

Place pasta on a platter. Pour sauce over the pasta and sprinkle with parsley and sautéed mushrooms. Grind fresh pepper over the dish and serve immediately.

Serves 4.

Note: Spiral noodles give the dish a festive look. Combine the pasta with a combination of small vegetables, like green peas, carrots, scallions sliced small, pour the sauce over the pasta, cover and bake 30 minutes at 350 degrees. Serve with warm challah dipped in olive oil and green salad.

~~~~~~~~~~~~~~~~~~~~~~~~~~~~~~~~~~~~

In the Moroccan Jewish community, if a new fruit appears in the marketplace during the week, it is purchased for eating on Shabbat, at which time the Sheheheyanu prayer is recited. There used to be a very interesting custom of having a pre-Shabbat snack of cake and radishes, which they called 'Bo't Kallah,' 'Welcome, Queen (Shabbat).'

Dr. Ron Wolfson, The Family Guide to Preparing for and Celebrating the Sabbath, p.243.

~MACARONI AND CHEESE~

If you've been wondering how to handle your children's envy for the macaroni and cheese their friends eat, here's the recipe you've been waiting for. Also tastes great at room temperature, or chilled the next day. You can make a special children's Shabbat from this recipe.

Preheat oven to 350°

2 vegetarian bouillon cubes
1 cup boiling water
1 medium onion chopped fine
8 Tablespoons soy margarine, divided in half
1 pound silken Tofu
2 Tablespoons spicy brown mustard
1 Tablespoon vegan Worcestershire Sauce
3 Tablespoons flour
1/4 teaspoon each sea salt and pepper
1 teaspoon Herbamare ®
1 teaspoon Old Bay® seasoning
1 teaspoon onion powder
1 teaspoon turmeric
2 Tablespoons soy or tamari sauce
1/2 cup whole wheat bread crumbs, mixed with
1/4 teaspoon nutritional yeast
8 ounces cooked elbow macaroni or spirals

Combine the bouillon and water and let sit. Sauté the onion in 4 tablespoons soy margarine, add salt and pepper

When onions become translucent, add the flour, stir constantly until smooth, add the vegetable bouillon liquid to the pan, stirring occasionally.

Meanwhile in food processor combine the silken tofu, mustard, Worcestershire sauce, tamari, Old Bay, Herbamare®, turmeric and onion powder and blend until smooth. Pour into the skillet with the flour gravy, mix and cook three minutes over a low flame.

(Continue)

Put the cooked and drained macaroni into a casserole dish and and pour in the sauce, stirring until all the macaroni is well coated.

Bake for 30 minutes, covered. Take the bread crumbs and add the remaining 4 tablespoons melted margarine, spread over the top, broil 3-5 minutes, cool ten minutes before serving.

If you refrain from trampling the Sabbath,
From pursuing your affairs on
On my holy day;
If you call the Sabbath "delight,"
The Lord's holy day "honored;'
And if you honor it and go not your ways
or look to your affairs, nor strike bargains--
then you can seek the favor of the lord.
I will set you astride the heights of the earth,
And let you enjoy the heritage of your father, Jacob

Isaiah

~~COOKED VEGETABLE DISHES~~
WITH OR WITHOUT GRAINS

Most of these dishes can easily become entrées when combined with a tofu, tempeh or seitan dish.

כשרות
Kashrut
Eating the Jewish Way

~ROASTED ROOT VEGETABLES WITH WINE SAUCE~

A fussy dish, but well worth the effort. This process maximizes flavor and the combination of vegetables are incredibly delicious made this way. Any that are left will
be good at room temperature on Saturday, but don't count on leftovers unless you
want to make a second pan and hide it until Saturday. (Save leftover water for
vegetable stock.) If vegetables are organic, do not peel except for sweet potatoes.

Pre-heat oven to 375°

> 3 golden beets, scrubbed
> 1 turnip, scrubbed, but not peeled, if organic
> 2 parsnips, scrubbed, but not peeled, if organic
> 2 large potatoes, do not peel if organic
> 3 carrots, scrubbed, but not peeled, if organic
> 3 medium or 2 large sweet potatoes, peeled
> 4 Tablespoons olive oil
> 8 shallot cloves
> 2 garlic cloves
> 2 teaspoons of a good prepared mustard
> 1/2 teaspoon cumin
> 1/3 cup red or white wine
> sea salt and pepper to taste

Bring a large soup pot of water to boil
Cut all the vegetables into large chunks and put the chunked vegetables in to the
boiling water in three or four batches. Boil 2-4 minutes for each batch. Take each
batch out and drain.
Put the olive oil into a large skillet. Mix wine, mustard and cumin. When oil is hot
(but not smoking), add the mixture of vegetables to the oil.
Add the root vegetables and the sliced shallots and garlic. Stir-fry until golden at the
edges. Combine wine with the mustard and cumin and add to the pan. Add salt and
pepper.
Transfer to a roasting pan and roast for 45 minutes. Turn every 10-15 minutes.
They should be golden and crispy.

Serves 6-8.

~SPICY BLACK BEANS AND SWEET POTATOES~

An odd combination, and note "spicy" in the description----take it seriously.

Preheat oven to 425 °
Step one

1 Tablespoon olive oil
1 medium sweet potato or butternut squash, peeled and diced into 1" cubes
1 small red bell pepper, membranes and seeds removed, diced small
1 small green bell pepper, membranes and seeds removed, diced small
1 teaspoon salt

Brush baking pan with oil. Toss vegetables together with the remaining oil and salt. Spread out in an even layer on pan. Roast until browned and tender, stirring frequently, about 25 to 30 minutes.

Step two

2 cups black beans, fresh cooked or canned
(drain liquid and rinse if using canned)
1 cup onions, diced small
2 cloves garlic, diced small
2 teaspoons chipotle chili in adobo or ground chipotle chili
(add more if you like it hotter, less for mild)
2 Tablespoons tamari
1/2 teaspoon salt
6 sprigs chopped cilantro or 1 teaspoon dried

If you are using beans that you have cooked, drain them of excess liquid. Pour them into a pot and toss together with the onion, garlic, chipotle, tamari, salt and cilantro. Warm on low and stir in the sweet potatoes and bell peppers.

Serves 6 to 8

Tip: Can be made into soup by adding water to the mixture, bring to a boil, turn down to simmer and season to taste.

~VEGETABLES IN SPICY MISO SAUCE~

Great summer Shabbat dish. Can be made on Thursday and save time on Friday. Chills well. Can also be made into a delicious entrée by adding 1/2 pound cooked whole wheat spaghetti or rice pasta to the pan, and warming together.

Step one

3 cups green beans or zucchini, wash, trim ends

1/2 teaspoon salt

Bring 2 quarts of water with salt to a boil Add vegetables and cook about 3 minutes. Drain through a colander and set aside.

Step two

1 Tablespoon toasted sesame oil

1 red onion, sliced thin

4 cloves garlic, minced

1 Tablespoon of capers (optional)

1 small red, yellow or orange bell pepper, seeded, ribs removed
and sliced into thin strips

Brush bottom of skillet with oil and toss in onions. Sauté for 1 minute then add garlic. Cook until onions are softened, then stir in bell pepper and cook for 5 minutes.

Step three

1 jalapeno pepper, seeds removed, or green salsa sauce

1 Tablespoon barley miso

1 Tablespoon maple syrup or agave syrup

4 teaspoons arrowroot flour

1 cup water

Toasted sesame seeds (optional)

Blend the jalapeno and miso in a food processor or blender.
Add maple syrup, arrowroot flour and the water and blend until well combined.
Add vegetables to the sauté pan and cook for 5 more minutes on medium heat.
Pour in the liquid ingredients and stir constantly until thickened, about 1 minute.
Pour into serving bowl and sprinkle with the sesame seeds.

Serves 4

~ROASTED GARLIC CLOVES~

Garlic is so healthy, but most of us avoid it because of its strong smell; however, roast it, bake it, and voila! a whole new taste and smell sensation. Here is an easy way to roast garlic. All you need is a ceramic garlic roaster and the conventional toaster oven, which most of us have. Put the garlic roaster in the toaster oven, set on 350 degrees or thereabouts, and roast the garlic until it is soft. Squish it out of its skin and mash it into the vegetable (preceding page) recipe---or any other recipe.

~~~~~~~

~MOROCCAN STYLE GREENS~

Simple and easy!

1 pound of greens--kale or suit yourself
some olive oil
some lemon juice

Cut up greens and sauté in a little olive oil with lemon juice or vinegar, a teaspoon ground cumin and one Tablespoon sweet Hungarian paprika.

~~~~~~~~~~~~~~~~

On the Shabbat night, there are many blessings, blessing over wine, blessing over bread, blessing over a new fruit, and family blessings. The first of the family blessings are for the children. The blessing for sons is very traditional. It is the blessing Jacob bestowed on his grandchildren, who were the children of Joseph: "May God make you like Ephraim and Menasseh." Daughters are blessed in the name of Sarah, Rebecca, Rachel and Leah.

~SPICY BROCCOLI RABE WITH MUSHROOMS~

Don't confuse broccoli with broccoli rabe---they belong to the same family, but the similarity ends there. If you haven't met the relative broccoli rabe yet, now is a good time.

Wash and cut the bottom few inches off broccoli stems as they tend to be tough and chewy. Coarsely chop the rest of the broccoli rabe in large pieces. Bring water to a rapid boil and drop in the broccoli. Cook only 30 seconds, or until bright in color. Remove from the water and drain.

1 bunch broccoli rabe
2 quarts water
1 Tablespoon olive oil
1 small onion, diced
2 cloves garlic, diced
1 cup sliced mushrooms
1/4 to 1/2 teaspoon red pepper flakes
(depending on how hot you like it)
Salt to taste
1 pound of wheat or rice pasta

Boil a large pot of water, and toss in the pasta. Cook 10 minutes, or according to directions of package

Heat oil in a sauté pan and add onion, cooking until onion is softened. Stir in garlic, cook another minute, then toss in mushrooms. Sauté 5 more minutes or until the mushrooms are browned. Mix in the broccoli and the red pepper flakes. Sprinkle with salt and cook 5 more minutes.
Drain the pasta and toss with the broccoli rabe mixture.

Serves 4-5

~ADJUKI BEAN POT~

A fast put-together dish for the Shabbat days when time runs out. Plan ahead. You can make two main ingredients in advance. The flavors in this dish can also be varied or enhanced.

1 1/2 cups of dry adjuki beans
2 Tablespoons olive oil
1 small eggplant, cut in chunks, with skin on
1 small leek, washed well,
                 chopped with green portion
2 bell peppers, one green, one red, cut in chunks
3 Tablespoons tomato paste
2 Tablespoons tamari sauce or Braggs liquid
1 teaspoon ground cumin
pinch of salt
1/2 block or 1/2 pound marinated tofu, cut in chunks
1 Tablespoon Dijon mustard

Prepare beans and marinated tofu in advance.

Place eggplant and cut peppers in a steamer, and steam until eggplant is soft but not mushy
While vegetables are cooking, oil a large skillet
On low-medium heat, sauté chopped leeks or onion.
Add beans, tomato paste, tamari or Braggs liquid and cumin. Heat, mix to stir in all the flavors. Cover, keep warm on low flame.

Oil small skillet and sauté prepared marinated tofu.
When vegetables are finished, add them to the beans in the skillet, add tofu to the beans, mix well.

Serves 6

Note: For a zippier taste, add a pinch of cayenne pepper and/or 1 Tablespoon of prepared Dijon mustard.

~WHITE BEAN AND VEGETABLE GRATIN~

The original French meaning of "gratin" is 'crusted' top.--not cheese. Made that way, this is a good recipe for vegans.

Preheat oven to 375°

2 cups green beans, cut in half
4 cups freshly cooked (or canned) small white beans
3 ripe tomatoes, quartered
1 small red onion, quartered vertically. Separate sections
1 yellow bell pepper, cored, cut into 1 inch cubes
5 garlic cloves, roughly chopped
1/4 cup olive oil
1 teaspoon chopped fresh thyme
        or 1/2 teaspoon dried thyme
Salt & freshly ground black pepper to taste

In a large bowl, combine green beans with remaining ingredients, except those set aside for the topping. Toss well, place in a 2-1/2 quart gratin dish or shallow casserole. Pat down the top to make smooth.

Topping
1 cup fresh bread crumbs (or toast 2 slices of bread)
1 Tablespoon olive oil

In a small bowl, combine bread crumbs with 1 Tablespoon oil, mix well. Spread crumbs over the green beans evenly. Cover dish with foil. Bake covered for 30 minutes. Remove foil, bake uncovered 30 more minutes. Let sit 10 minutes before serving.

Serves 4
Note: Navy or great northern beans can also be used. If using canned beans, rinse. Steam green beans about 5 minutes until crunchy, but not tender. Use toasted matzoh farvel for Pesach Shabbat dinner.

~LENTIL AND BULGUR SALAD~

Can be served as a main dish or as a side dish. If served as a side dish, goes well with sautéed apples and seitan steaks. Serve as main dish in stuffed green pepper for a festive look.

2 cups fine-grain bulgur
3 cups boiling water
2 cups brown lentils, rinsed
4 cups vegetable broth or water
8-10 scallions, chopped
1 large potato, sweet potato or yam, peeled and
cut into 1-inch cubes, boiled until tender
1 bunch spinach, lightly steamed and chopped
    or 1 10-ounce box frozen chopped spinach,
defrosted
3/4 cup toasted walnuts or pine nuts
Vinaigrette dressing (recipe below)

Place bulgur in medium bowl. Pour the boiling water over the bulgur and let stand for 30 minutes. Place in colander and squeeze out excess water.

In medium pot, bring the vegetable broth or water to a boil and add the lentils. Reduce the heat and let simmer, covered, for about 30 minutes or until lentils are tender, but not mushy. Drain if necessary.

In a large bowl, combine the bulgur and lentils. Add the scallions, potato, spinach, and nuts, and mix well.

Add the vinaigrette dressing, stir well, and serve immediately or refrigerate until ready to serve.

(Continue)

Vinaigrette Dressing

4 cloves garlic, minced
1 heaping teaspoon Dijon mustard
1 teaspoon sugar
1 teaspoon salt
ground black pepper to taste
1/2 cup balsamic vinegar
2/3 cup olive oil

Whisk together the first six ingredients in a small bowl.

Slowly add the olive oil, whisking constantly, until all ingredients are thoroughly combined. Adjust seasonings to taste.

Serves 8-12

Note: If serving as main dish in stuffed green peppers, remember to have 8-12 peppers on hand and a large casserole dish to place them in. Cover to seal in moisture.

~~~~~~~~~~~~~~~~~~~~~~~~~~~~~~~~~~~~

I view the Sabbath as a surcease from and a protest against all forms of competition, even when they come in attractive packages marked 'self advancement' or 'self improvement.' I view the Sabbath in this respect as a 'useless' day. Our forefathers had a keen understanding of the fact that sleep on the Sabbath day was a form of coming closer to God. We must once again understand that doing nothing, being silent and open to the world, letting things happen inside can be as important as, and sometimes more important than what we commonly call the useful

W. Gunter Plaut, "The Sabbath As Protest"

~KOREAN STYLE BARLEY SALAD~

Like white bean stew, this dish can also be prepared in advance and chilled. Good for working cooks. Note that the dressing *is* spicy. Can be served at room temperature or chilled. and will keep until Saturday. So if you're expecting company for Saturday lunch or for a Havdala meal, double the recipe.

5 cups vegetable broth or water
1-1/2 cups pearled barley
1/2 cup matchstick-cut carrots
1/2 cup matchstick-cut red or green pepper
2/3 cup sliced scallion
1 cup sliced white mushrooms
Soy sauce-sesame dressing (recipe below)

Bring water or broth to boil in medium pot. Cook mushrooms in the water. Add the barley, cover, and simmer over low heat for 40 minutes or until tender. Drain excess water if necessary. Transfer cooked barley to a serving bowl, add the vegetables and mix well.

Pour dressing over salad and mix well. Chill until ready to serve.

Soy Sauce-Sesame Dressing

1/4 cup soy sauce
1 Tablespoon brown sugar, packed
1/4 cup dark sesame oil
2 Tablespoons toasted sesame seeds
2 cloves garlic, minced
2 Tablespoons rice vinegar
1-2 teaspoons chili garlic sauce* or to taste

(Continue)

Heat soy sauce in a small pot until hot, but not boiling.

Remove soy sauce from heat, add the sugar and stir until dissolved. Add remaining ingredients and mix well.

Serves 6

Note*: Chili garlic sauce is available in the Asian section of many large supermarkets. If unavailable, substitute hot sauce or cayenne pepper to taste, but be careful using these ingredients.
Also, since barley is one of the Seven Sacred Species of Israel mentioned in the Bible, this would be a nice dish to serve at a TuB'shevat seder.

~~~~~~~~~~~~~~~~~~~~~~~~~~~~~~~

"There is not any city of the Grecians, nor any of the Barbarians, nor any nation whatsoever, whither our custom of resting on the seventh day hath not come!" Josephus (edited by Dennys), Vol 4, Nos 7, 8, p.100.

~~~~~~~~~~

The seventh day is a festival, not of this or of that city, but of the universe.
Philo of Alexandria, "Notes and Queries," Vol. 4, 99

~BOK CHOY WITH LEMON TAHINI SAUCE~

A taste of Asian cooking for the Shabbat. If you are unacquainted with umeboshi vinegar or umeboshi paste, now is the time to find out about these remarkable condiments, made from plum skins. Expensive, yes, but not really because you use only a small amount of this condiment. The vegetable is great served over a grain, rice or pasta. See suggestion at end of recipe.

1 large head bok choy or 2 small, washed and chopped into bite size pieces
1/4 teaspoon salt

Fill pot with water and salt and bring to a boil. Cook the bok choy until bright green, remove from pot and drain.

1/2 cup tahini
3/4 cup hot water
1 Tablespoon umeboshi plum vinegar
1 Tablespoon lemon juice
1/2 teaspoon toasted sesame oil
2 cloves garlic, minced

Pour all the ingredients into the food processor and whip until creamy, Pour over bok choy and serve.

Serves 4--or 6 if served over pasta or rice.

Suggestion: Any hardy green vegetable can be used with this sauce including broccoli. Serve over brown rice or toss it with shell noodles and peas and bake covered in the oven for 15 minutes. You will have to double the recipe if you want to bake the sauce with the pasta.

~EGGPLANT AND SUMAC STEW~

This is a good recipe for a small Shabbat dinner. If there are only two for Shabbat, there will be a good leftover for two for Shabbat lunch the next day. Also, good as an accompaniment to a vegetable or lentil loaf.

2 Tablespoons olive oil
1 medium onion, chopped
3-4 garlic cloves, sliced
1 medium eggplant, cut into 3/4 inch cubes
1-1/2 Tablespoons tomato paste
1 teaspoon ground sumac
1/4 teaspoon cinnamon
1/4 teaspoon sugar
1 cup water
1 teaspoon salt
pinch of cayenne pepper

Heat the olive oil in a large skillet over medium heat. Add onion and cook until it begins to brown.

Add the garlic and cook one minute. Add in the cubed eggplant and cook for another minute.

Mix in the tomato paste, sumac, cinnamon, and sugar, stirring well to distribute the tomato paste throughout the mixture.

Add the water and bring the mixture to a boil. Cover the pan and let the mixture simmer over low heat until the eggplant is soft, but not mushy, about 20 minutes.

Add salt and cayenne to taste.

Serves 4

~SESAME BROCCOLI~

Perhaps Bush Senior wouldn't eat it, but many people who don't care for vegetables like this dish which can be served hot or cold.

Eat greens every day. Scientists are madly trying to extract the anti-oxidants from vegetables and fruit so they can be put in a pill or powder. Some of these concoctions are already on the market. But nutrients are meant to be absorbed from their source. Eat real food daily. Don't discard the stalks of broccoli. They are very healthful.

One large bunch fresh broccoli. Cut off and separate the florets.
You can use some of the stalk too, scrape the outer coarse skin and slice fine.
1 teaspoon olive oil
1 red, yellow or orange pepper, sliced into matchsticks.
1-2 cloves of garlic, crushed
2 Tablespoons lightly toasted sesame seeds
1 Tablespoon dark sesame oil
A few splashes of tamari sauce (or shoyu)

Steam the broccoli until just tender-crisp and transfer to a bowl. If using some of the stalks, steam these a bit longer---they take longer to cook.
Lightly toast sesame seeds in a skillet, stir over low heat.
Sauté (sweat) pepper and garlic. Add the garlic after the pepper is soft.

Add the pepper and garlic to the broccoli, then add the other ingredients.
Toss until mixed.

Serve hot with rice or cold as finger food and appetizer

You can use the same recipes with steamed or lightly sautéed greens, such as collards or kale.
Serve over brown rice or millet

~BROCCOLI WITH SPICY MUSTARD DILL SAUCE~

There are many choices today in mustards--sweet, spicy or otherwise, but if you cannot find a spicy mustard, add a pinch of cayenne to whatever mustard you have. Eden Foods sells a horseradish mustard that is very good and available at most natural food stores--or you can make your own.

1/2 cup extra firm tofu
1/4 cup nondairy milk
1 Tablespoon spicy mustard
1 teaspoon umeboshi plum vinegar
1 Tablespoon olive oil
1 garlic clove, chopped
2 Tablespoons fresh parsley coarsely chopped
1 Tablespoon fresh dill or 1 teaspoon dried dill
1 head of broccoli
1/2 teaspoon salt

Blend the first eight ingredients in food processor or blender until creamy.

Wash broccoli and cut into flowerets. Cut off the tough bottom part of the stem and peel the remaining stem with a peeler or knife. Slice into rounds.

Bring a pot of water to a rapid boil. Add salt and drop in broccoli. Cook until bright and tender, about 3 minutes. Remove to colander or strainer and shake off excess water. Arrange on a platter or bowl and pour sauce over.

Serves 4.

~POTATO AND WILD RICE CAKES ~
~WITH WALNUT SAGE SAUCE~

NOT YOUR BUBBE'S LATKES!

Pam Brown brought these to a festival that the Mid-Hudson Vegetarian Society hosted in Rhinebeck, NY. They flew off the tray. Excellent for a Channuka Shabbat.

Preheat oven to 400°

Step one

> 2 teaspoons olive oil
> 1 small onion, minced
> 2 cloves garlic, minced

Warm oil in skillet and add onions. Cook for 2 minutes, then add garlic. Sauté until the onions are very brown, almost caramelized.

Step two

> 1/2 cup wild rice
> 3 cups water
> 4 cups baking potatoes, peeled and cut in chunks
> Pinch of salt

Wash rice and bring water and salt to a boil. Add rice, bring back to a boil then turn to low, cover and cook 45 minutes. Drain well and set aside. While the rice is cooking, bring another pot of water to a boil and cook potatoes until tender, approximately 15 to 20 minutes then drain.

Step three

> 2 Tablespoons olive oil
> Spray of olive oil
> Salt and pepper to taste

Mix together potatoes and onions and mash well with a potato masher. Drizzle in the olive oil and season with salt and pepper. Combine well with the rice and form into 5" patties 1/2 " thick. Coat a skillet with olive oil and cook patties until brown. Flip over and brown on the other side. Serve as is or with the following sauce:

(Continue)

Sauce:

3/4 cup toasted walnuts
1/2 cup parsley, finely chopped
2 Tablespoon olive oil
1/2 cup water
1/2 tsp. ground sage
1 clove garlic, minced

Grind walnuts in the food processor. Add the rest of the ingredients and blend until creamy.
Drizzle a little sauce on each potato-rice cake.

Or serve in the old-fashioned way with applesauce or vegan sour cream.

~~~~~~~~~~~~~~~~~~~~~~~~~~~~~~~~~~~~~

The custom on Friday afternoon
is to taste each of the foods
prepared for Shabbat to make certain
that they are all properly cooked and tasty.

(Mishna Beruriah250:4)

Make your children the Shabbat tasters

~HERB BAKED BROWN RICE AND SPINACH~
~WITH ALMOND TOPPING~

 A three-step process for the hostess with leisure time, but worth the effort any time.

Preheat oven to 350 °
Step one

2 teaspoons olive oil
1 medium leek, diced small (only the white part)
2 cloves garlic, chopped
1 cup carrots, diced
1 cup celery, diced
1 bunch spinach, washed and chopped
1/2 teaspoon salt

Leeks can be very sandy, so always wash the leek carefully by slicing in half and rinsing in between all the leaves. Warm oil in a skillet and add leeks, cook until bright, about 2 minutes. Stir in garlic and cook another minute, then mix in the carrots and celery. Sauté for 3 minutes, toss in spinach and sprinkle with salt and simmer for one more minute.

Step two

4 cups cooked brown rice
1 large or 2 small bay leaves
1/2 teaspoon dried marjoram or 2 teaspoons. fresh
1 teaspoon dried thyme or 2 teaspoons. fresh
1 cup water or stock
2 Tablespoons tamari

Mix all of the above together in the pan with the vegetables and stir until well combined. Oil a baking dish that has a lid, then spoon in the mixture. Smooth with a spatula, cover and bake 30 minutes.

(*Continue*)

Topping

3/4 cup whole wheat pastry flour
1/2 cup coarsely ground almonds
1/4 cup olive oil
1 to 2 Tablespoons water
1/2 teaspoon dried oregano
1 teaspoon dried parsley
or 1 Tablespoon chopped fresh parsley
1/2 teaspoon salt

Turn the oven temperature up to 400°.
Mix the flour and nuts together. Add the oil, stir thoroughly, then drizzle in the 2 Tablespoons of water. The mixture should look moist but not wet. Squeeze a small amount in your hand to see if it holds together. If it is dry and crumbly, add another Tablespoon of water. Sprinkle over rice 15 minutes before it is done and bake without a cover until brown. Remove the bay leaves before serving.

Serves 4-6

Note: Substitute the crumb topping with sliced fresh tomatoes over the entire top, or place tomato slices under the crumb topping, and bake until the tomatoes are soft but not mushy.

~~~~~~

Light a candle
Drink wine.
Softly the Sabbath has plucked
the sinking sun.
Slowly the Sabbath descends
the rose of heaven in her hand

Light a Candle, by Zelda, Israeli poet. Trans. by Marcia Falk.

~POLENTA TART WITH~
~CARAMELIZED MUSHROOM SAUCE~

Tarts are fussy to make, but they make a Shabbat table look festive. This recipe makes 8-10 tarts which could be enough for Saturday lunch as well.

Preheat oven to 400 °

Step one

> 3 cups water or stock
> 1 Tablespoon olive oil
> 1 teaspoon basil, dried
> 1 teaspoon Earth Balance
> 1 cup corn grits
> Salt and fresh ground pepper to taste

Bring water or stock to a boil. Pour in the olive oil, basil and Earth Balance. Whisk in the corn grits in a steady stream. Continue whisking until well combined and thickened. Turn down to a low simmer, cover and stir frequently. Cook for 20 minutes or until cornmeal pulls away from the sides of the pot.

Step two

> Spray of olive oil
> 2 teaspoons tamari

Oil the bottom and sides of an 8" tart pan, cake pan, or any small baking dish. Pour cornmeal mixture into pan and smooth top till even. Brush with olive oil and tamari. Bake in oven for 20 minutes or until slightly brown. Set aside.

Step three

> Spray of olive oil
> 1 teaspoon olive oil
> 1 medium onion, diced
> 2 cloves garlic, chopped
> 2 cups mushrooms, sliced
> 1/2 teaspoon salt
> 2 cups chopped fresh tomatoes, peeled, seeded and
> diced or 1 14.5 oz canned chopped tomatoes, drained
> 1/2 teaspoon dried oregano or a few sprigs fresh
> 10 leaves basil, fresh chopped or 1 teaspoon dried
> Salt and fresh ground black pepper to taste

(Continue)

Brush bottom of sauté pan with oil. Add onions and garlic and cook for a minute, just until softened.

Toss in mushrooms and sauté until tender on medium heat. Sprinkle with salt. The mushrooms will give off water but for best flavor, sauté until the water has cooked away and the mushrooms are brown and caramelized

Add tomatoes and cook until tender if raw, or until warmed if canned.

Sprinkle with the oregano, and basil and season with salt and pepper.

Invert the pan containing the cooled polenta onto a platter and top with sauce.
Cut in wedges and serve.

Serves 8-10

Note: Avoid the instant polenta that is in supermarkets as it lacks flavor and texture.

~KASHA JAMBOREE~

Many people carry a life-long prejudice against kasha from their childhood, because it was usually one of those foods Mom used to say, "Eat it, it's good for you," and then serve an overcooked, dried-out plate of kasha. But kasha is good for you, especially for diabetics because it has lots of fiber. There are simple rules for making kasha moist and delicious. It can also be made into a festive holiday dish when other ingredients are added to it.

To make plain kasha, follow these simple rules:

2 cups of buckwheat groats, rinsed

2 Tablespoons olive oil

4 cups boiling water

2 vegetable bouillon cubes or 1 Tablespoon vegetal.

Heat olive oil in a medium size skillet over a medium light, add groats, mix thoroughly to coat groats with oil, and brown slightly.
Meanwhile, boil the water and add bouillon cubes or vegetal.
Add the boiling water to groats carefully, as water might splash. Turn down heat to low, cover, and cook about 15 minutes. Uncover and fluff with a fork.

In another large skillet heat 2-3 Tablespoons oil and lightly sauté the following:

1/2 large green pepper, cut into 1/2 inch pieces

1/2 large yellow or red pepper, cut into 1/2 inch pieces

Add

3 scallions, cut into 1/2 pieces

1 cup frozen corn niblets

Toss cooked kasha into skillet with the cooked vegetables for a colorful dish

Serves 6-8

Variations: Add green peas and/or carrots, and for an even more festive dish, replace vegetables with cooked apricots or dehydrated cranberries and/or apples, or any combination of these.

~BROWN RICE WITH MUSHROOM SAUCE ~

Step One

2 Tablespoons olive oil
1 small onion, finely diced
2 cloves garlic, minced
1 cup button mushrooms, sliced thin (about 4 large or 8 small)
1/2 teaspoon salt

Brush bottom of skillet with oil. Starting with the onions, sauté for 1 minute, then add garlic. Cook until translucent, then stir in mushrooms and salt. Sauté until mushrooms are brown and caramelized and all of the liquid is gone, about 15 to 20 minutes.

Step Two

1/4 cup unbleached white flour or 1/4 cup whole wheat four
2 teaspoons margarine
1 cup water
1 cup nondairy milk
1/4 teaspoon thyme (optional)
1 teaspoon tamari
Salt and pepper to taste
4 cups cooked brown rice
1/4 cup chopped parsley
Dash of paprika

Stir in flour and margarine and coat vegetables. Whisk in water and milk, stirring briskly until well combined. Turn heat to low and cook 10 to 15 minutes, stirring frequently until flour is cooked and loses its raw taste.

If it is too thick, add more liquid. Place a heat deflector underneath if you have one. Add salt and pepper.

Mound rice onto plate and pour sauce over it. Sprinkle with the parsley and paprika.

Serves 4.

(Continue for sauce)

Sauce

Spray of olive oil
1 teaspoon olive oil
1 medium onion, diced
2 cloves garlic, minced
1 cup mushrooms, diced
2 ribs celery, diced
2 medium carrots diced
1/2 cup fresh or frozen corn
1/2 cup fresh or frozen peas
1 teaspoon ground sage
2 Tablespoons tamari
1/2 teaspoon salt
1/2 cup water

Wipe a small casserole dish with oil. Warm a skillet with oil, add the onions. Sauté a few minutes, add garlic and cook another minute. Stir in the rest of the vegetables, cook until slightly tender. Mix in the barley and sprinkle with the sage, tamari, salt and the 1/2 cup of water. Cover, bake for 35 minutes, or until the barley is bubbling. While the barley is cooking, make the bread crumbs. You can use stale bread, process into crumbs and store in a jar in your freezer, and always have bread crumbs on hand.

3 slices whole grain dried bread
(fresh bread will not make crumbs)
1 Tablespoon fresh parsley, finely chopped or 1 teaspoon dried
1/2 teaspoon dried thyme
pinch of salt
Spray or sprinkle of olive oil

Remove bread crusts and tear or cut into small pieces. Pulse in the food processor into coarse crumbs. Toss with parsley and salt and spray with olive oil. Top the barley with the bread crumbs and bake uncovered until the crumbs are brown the last 10 minutes.

Serves 4 to 6.

SOUPS
As An Entrée---Or Preceding The Entrée

Soup is the true comfort food, and for many cultures soup is the main dish, surrounded with a variety of smaller dishes. Western people organize their meals around one major dish called the entrée. But it is not necessary to organize a meal this way, and it is interesting to organize it in other ways. Vietnamese people, for example, eat soup as their major dish, usually a whopping big soup dish---almost like our cholent. As you look over these soups, think of one or two as a main dish with a variety of appetizers, a kind of dim sum served on a large tray or a lazy Susan. Many cultures serve a variety of small dishes, such as the Dutch Indonesians who pass around many dishes, instead of having a central dish. These can be organized around soup as the main dish. Try this most interesting way to serve a Shabbat dinner. The advantage of soup as an entrée is that soup can be made in advance, time enhances the flavors and it can be frozen---so easy to serve for a Shabbat meal.

Delicious, easy to make and full of nourishing ingredients, soups can be put together from leftovers or made from scratch. As long as you have onions and a few vegetables you have soup. The possibilities are endless. Soup can be made with vegetables, grains, beans or a combination of all. A great virtue of soup is that it freezes well. Make up a soup pot, and freeze individual portions ahead of time for the Shabbat dinner. Voila! You have the first--or the main--or the second course--depending on how you want to arrange it.

Vegetable stock is often a mystery to people, but it is simple to prepare, and can be made from any vegetable scraps and frozen in portions. On the other hand, you can make excellent soups without stock--but for the perfectionist, here are some suggestions for soup stock:

Save the ends, tops and trimmings of vegetables you use during the week. Six cups of leftover vegetables will make 4 cups of stock. Before cooking, pick out vegetables that are yellow, wilted or look inedible. Coarsely chop and rinse well in a colander. Cover vegetables with water in a soup pot and bring to medium simmer and cook about 45 minutes to one hour. Once the vegetables are very soft, strain through a sieve. (Don't let the vegetables sit in their liquid, because bitter flavors can result.) After the stock is strained, cool and freeze in containers in amounts you would normally use.

To intensify the stock flavors, boil the stock down to a few cups. All the soup recipes can be made with water and will turn out fine. With a few guidelines, stock will enhance the flavor.

Vegetables that have strong flavors will dominate the taste, while others that are too bitter should not be included. **Don't include**

> Beets and beet greens
> Bitter tasting greens like kale
> Turnips and rutabagas
> Red cabbage
> Green cabbage
> Broccoli and cauliflower
> Red and green peppers

After the stock has cooled, strain through a piece of cheesecloth. Start stocks with very cold water as cold water draws out any dirt or debris in the vegetables, causing debris to rise to the top. Watch as stock cooks to skim off any foam or murky looking water.

Start vegetable stock with onions, carrots and celery and add other vegetables of your choice. (Some people use the onion skins in stocks.)

Some of the best soups are made with leftover cooked vegetables, grains or beans combined together. Using leftover grains such as white Basmati rice, cooked barley or potatoes that are puréed with water or non-dairy milk makes a delicious cream soup. Add the cooked grain to a small pot, cover with water, bring to a boil, turn low to simmer until the grain becomes creamy. Use a blender to create a smooth, rich and velvety texture. The wand blender, which can be immersed right into the soup pot, is an excellent kitchen tool.

Grains such as quinoa, bulgur, kasha or couscous <u>do not</u> lend themselves well for blending into cream soups. They often overwhelm the taste and add an aftertaste.

A little garnish or topping adds texture and flavor, especially for creamy soups which can be a little flat without a splash of color or crunch. Garnishes can be as simple as chopped fresh parsley, scallions, cilantro or a sprinkle of ground nuts, chopped raw vegetables, roasted pepper puree, etc.

There is also commercial vegetable stock which can be bought, or a simple stock made from water and one or two vegetable bouillon cubes.

~ROASTED VEGETABLE STOCK~

Roasting the vegetables gives this stock a rich, full bodied flavor. Cutting the vegetables into small pieces, about 1/4 inch, exposes more of the surface, allowing for browning and caramelization.
Note: Made in two steps

Preheat oven to 425°

Step One:

> Olive oil
> 1 leek, coarsely chopped
> 2 cups carrots, cut in chunks
> 2 celery ribs, cut in large pieces
> 1 large yellow or white onion, quartered
> 1 cup button mushrooms
> 1 teaspoon. salt
> 2 Tablespoons tamari soy sauce
> 2 Tablespoons olive oil

Wash leeks carefully. Cut in half, separate the leaves and rinse between the leaves. Spray a baking sheet with oil. Toss all of the above ingredients together with salt, tamari and oil. Spread out in one even layer on the pan. (Make sure that vegetables are not piled on top of each other or they will steam instead of roasting.) Roast until tender, about 30 minutes. Stir frequently.

Step Two:

> 6 cups cold water
> 2 bay leaves
> 4 cloves garlic
> 1/2 cup chopped parley

Pour water into the soup pot and bring to a boil. Turn down to medium and add the vegetables, bay leaves and garlic. Simmer for 30 minutes, add parsley and cook 5 minutes more. Cool and strain.

Yields about 6 cups.

~MUSHROOM STOCK~

Excellent for brothy soups, for mushroom soup, hot and sour soup or to add a deep mushroom flavor to any other soup or sauce. **Note**: Made in two steps.

Step one:

> 2 cups button mushrooms, sliced
> 6 dried shitake mushrooms, sliced
> 1 teaspoon olive oil
> 1 medium onion, diced
> 1 teaspoon dry sweetener
> 1 leek, washed carefully and sliced
> 2 stalks celery, diced
> 1/2 teaspoon salt

Clean button mushrooms by wiping with a towel. If they are very dirty, fill a bowl with cold water, dunk mushrooms quickly, stirring with hand. Drain, pat dry and slice.

Soak shitakes in warm water to cover for 20 minutes or until soft enough to cut. Save the soaking water and strain through a mesh strainer or a piece of cheesecloth.

Brush the bottom of a soup pot with oil and warm the pot. Add onions, sauté for 5 minutes on medium heat. Sprinkle with the sweetener and cook until the onions start to brown. Stir in the mushrooms, leek and celery, sprinkle with salt and cook another 5 minutes.

Step two

> 5 cups cold water
> 4 sprigs of thyme or 1/2 teaspoon. dried
> 2 Tablespoons tamari soy sauce
> Salt and pepper to taste

Pour water and mushroom soaking water into the pot and bring to a boil. Turn down to simmer for 45 minutes. Add thyme the last 10 minutes. Cool and strain out the vegetables.

Yield 5 to 6 cups. Boil down to 3 cups for a deeper flavor

~GOLDEN GLOW SHABBAT SOUP~

This is a great vegetarian substitute for the chicken soup that everyone expects for a Shabbat dinner--and it is healthier. It is another classic recipe from *The Jewish Vegetarian Year Cookbook*. Serve with toasted barley for more taste or with chopped parsley for color.

1 pound package yellow split peas (2 cups dry)
1 cup grated parsnips
1 cup grated carrots
Salt to taste
3 bay leaves

Cook yellow split peas according to directions on package.

Halfway through cooking time, add parsnips, carrots, salt and bay leaves.

Simmer with partially covered lid. Remove bay leaves before serving.

For a golden color and smoother taste, purée.

Serves 8.

~TOMATO SURPRISE SOUP~

This is a low-fat soup with high protein from the beans and lots of good phyto-chemicals from the cauliflower. The beans should be cooked first with kombu. (See section on cooking rice and beans.)

1 cup cooked cannolini beans (or other white beans)
one-half head of cauliflower
1 28 ounce can plum tomatoes
1/2 of a large onion or one small onion, diced
1 clove garlic diced
1 teaspoon olive oil
2 teaspoons sweet Hungarian Paprika
1/2 teaspoon each: dried basil, oregano, sea salt
1/8 teaspoon Cayenne pepper
2 bay leaves
1 teaspoon red wine vinegar

Steam the cauliflower in a small amount of water

Sauté the onion and garlic, first in a little water, then add the oil

Squeeze the juice from the tomatoes and place in a one and one-half quart pot.

Puree the tomatoes, beans, cauliflower, onion/garlic and the seasonings, except the bay leaf.

Add the puréed mixture to the liquid in the pot, add the bay leaf and vinegar and simmer gently at least 20 minutes to blend flavors.

Serves four, but recipe can easily be doubled to serve eight.

Suggestions: Serve garnished with sliced scallion tops. Could also be topped with some nutritional yeast for extra B12 value

~COLD CURRIED GREEN PEA SOUP~

Chilled soups are lovely to serve for a summer Shabbat evening and curried chilled green pea soup makes for a nice surprise soup.

> 1 teaspoon olive oil
> 1 pound package (2 cups dry) split green peas
> 4 cups of water
> 1 medium onion chopped
> 1 rib of celery chopped
> 2 teaspoons prepared curry
> Pinch of salt

Oil a large soup pot. Sauté onions and celery for about five minutes on low heat.
Rinse peas, put in a pot. Add water. Bring to a boil, lower the heat, cover and simmer for about 40 minutes. Add salt and curry. Puree in pot. Adjust seasonings.

Serves 6-8

~~~~~~~~~~~~~~~~~~~~~~

You would not think of time as having a texture, yet in a traditional Jewish household it becomes almost palpable. On Shabbat, I can almost feel the difference in the air I breathe, in the way the incandescent lamps give off light in my living room, in the way the children's skins glow, or the way the trees sway. Immediately after I light my candles, it is as if I flicked a switch that turned Shabbat on in the world.
                    Blu Greenberg, Shabbat

~GINGERED LENTIL SOUP~

It's rare that a hearty soup can also be described as elegant.

1 Tablespoon olive oil
1 package of lentils, rinsed
water to cover lentils about three inches
3 ribs of celery
three medium size carrots
1-1/2 teaspoons of ginger powder/
or 1 teaspoon of fresh grated ginger, or to taste
pinch of salt

Heat olive oil in large soup pot over low heat

Chop celery, put in pot to sauté. Chop carrots, add to pot

Add lentils and cover with water about three inches deep

Bring water to boil, lower heat, cook about 40 minutes until lentils are cooked
Add the ginger and salt. Mix well. Taste, adjust seasoning.

Serves 8

While the Sabbath is no cure-all for family ills, it can provide a glimpse of what family life can be at its best, as well as an opportunity to share a profound experience which binds all participants in a common framework of meaning.

Michael S. Kogan, Kingdom Present

~DOUBLE LENTIL SOUP~

There are many ingredients in this soup, but it cooks up fast and is easy to prepare. A very satisfying soup for a winter Shabbat, it is so hearty, that a small serving can start a Shabbat dinner or serve as a main dish with salad, challah and dips.

10 cups water
1 cup dried red lentils, washed
1/2 cup dried French lentils, washed
1/3 cup barley
1 and 1/2 inch piece kombu
1 large onion, diced
2 stalks celery, diced
2 cloves garlic, diced
3 carrots, sliced
2 small Yukon gold potatoes, diced
2 cups green cabbage, sliced fine
2 teaspoons cumin
1/2 teaspoon turmeric
2 Tablespoons Tamari or Braggs
1 Tablespoon Herbamare ®
1 Tablespoon olive oil
1 Tablespoon red apple cider vinegar
1 teaspoon brown mustard

Bring the water to a simmer. Add lentils, barley and kombu to the water. Don't add anything else until the lentils and barley are done. The red lentils will form a puree while the French Lentils and barley will stay separate.

Sauté onion first in a bit of water, then in the oil. When onions are soft add the celery and the garlic. Add to soup pot when the lentils are done (about one half hour). Add the rest of the ingredients, except the cider and the mustard. Simmer another half hour to blend the flavors.
Add vinegar and mustard at the end---a good way to finish a bean soup.

Servings: 12 small or 6 large

~DIJON ONION SOUP WITH HERB CROUTONS~

Sounds odd, but tastes great. Made in three steps, it's fun to make and serve on a cold Shabbat evening. The spices will warm up your guests.

Preheat oven to 450°

Step one:

> 1 Tablespoon olive oil
>
> 3 pounds white onions, sliced very thin
>
> 1 teaspoon sweetener
>
> 2 Tablespoons Dijon mustard
>
> 1 teaspoon salt

Warm oil in heavy soup pot and add onions stirring well to coat the onions with the oil. Sauté on medium high heat for 5 minutes, then add the sweetener and mustard. Continue cooking on medium heat for 10 minutes stirring frequently. When the onions are softened and browned, turn on very low, cover pot with a tight fitting lid and cook 15 more minutes. Sprinkle with salt, and cook another 20 to 30 minutes, stirring often. The longer you cook the onions, the sweeter and more delicious they become.

Step two

> 6 cups stock or water
>
> 1 teaspoon thyme
>
> 2 small bay leaves
>
> 3 Tablespoons tamari

Pour stock and seasonings into the pot. Bring to a low boil, turn down and simmer 10 minutes.

(Continue)

Step three:

>2 slices bread, (French, Italian or some type of rustic bread is best)
>1 teaspoon oregano
>1 teaspoon thyme
>1/2 teaspoon paprika
>2 Tablespoons olive oil
>2 Tablespoons parsley, minced
>Spray of olive oil

Cut bread into small cubes. Mix the herbs, paprika and parsley together. Toss the bread cubes with the olive oil and toss with the herbs, mixing well. Spread out on an oiled baking sheet or cover pan with a piece of parchment and bake until brown and crunchy, about 10 minutes, stirring frequently. Ladle soup into the bowls and drop in a few croutons.

Serves 6 to 8

Suggestion: Whisk in 1/4 cup unbleached flour after you have poured in the stock and continue whisking until well blended with the stock. Cook for 15 minutes or more. This produces a light creamy onion soup. The croutons will taste and work better if you let the bread cubes dry out a little bit. Do this step first so that they will be ready for baking while the soup is cooking.

~~~~~~~~~~~~~~~~~~~~~~~~~~~

HaShem said to Moses, "I have a precious gift in my treasury.
Shabbat is its name. Now go and tell Israel, I will present it to them"
Masechet Shabat 10b

~WHITE BEAN SOUP W/PARSLEY SUNFLOWER PESTO~

Another soup from Pam Brown, bursting with flavor

1 1/2 cups dry cannelloni or chickpeas, washed and cooked for two hours
4 cups cold water

Step one:

1 teaspoon olive oil
1 medium onion, chopped
3 cloves garlic, minced
2 stalks celery, diced
2 carrots, diced
2 cups tomatoes, diced
1 bay leaf
2 Tablespoons tamari
Salt and pepper to taste

Brush pot with oil and warm. Add onions and cook until tender, about 5 minutes. Stir in the garlic and cook another minute, then add the rest of the vegetables. After 5 minutes pour in the cooked beans with the liquid, the bay leaf and tamari. Bring to a medium boil and simmer for 15 minutes. Remove the bay leaf and season with salt and pepper.

Step two:

1/2 cup toasted sunflower seeds
1 1/2 cups packed fresh parsley leaves
2 garlic cloves
2 Tablespoons olive oil
1/4 cup water

To toast the sunflower seeds, heat a heavy skillet. Add seeds and toast stirring constantly until they turn brown and emit a nutty aroma, about 5 minutes.
Cool. Add parsley, garlic and sunflower seeds to the food processor. Pulse until well combined and roughly ground.
Slowly pour in the oil and the water into processor and blend until creamy.
Ladle soup into bowls and garnish with a dollop of pesto.
Serves 6.

~ELEGANT BROCCOLI SOUP~

Few people know that the husks of broccoli are very nutritious. We tend to use only the florets because they are easier to cook and they look pretty, but soup is one place where you can make use of those nutritious husks. Pare them first to remove the most fibrous part, and chop finely in a processor so that they will cook up at the same time as the more malleable florets.

Lightly oil large soup pot
1-1/2 cup onions chopped
1 rib of celery chopped
1 large head of broccoli
1 teaspoon nutmeg, or to taste
Pinch of salt
4 1/2 cups water
1/2 block of firm tofu
1/2 cup lightly toasted slivered almonds

Purée celery and chopped onions about five minutes in oiled pot
Pare the broccoli stalks and cut stalks into small pieces.
Add broccoli florets and stalks to pot
Add the water, cover the pot, bring to a boil, lower flame, simmer about 40 minutes. Purée for a smoother taste.

Serves 6

Variations: Add 1/2 pound of tofu to the soup to thicken it and make it creamy. This also gives you protein and vegetables in one dish. If you add tofu, drain moisture from it, and purée the tofu before adding to the soup. Add tofu to soup ten minutes before it is done. Then purée the whole soup.

Suggestions: For a sweeter taste, replace onions with a cup and half of scrubbed, chopped parsnip. Sauté together with celery. You may decide not to include the tofu if you use the parsnip, since both together would make the soup quite thick---unless, of course, you like very thick soup.
Sprinkle toasted almonds on top, or a dash of nutmeg.

~GINGERED CAULIFLOWER AND CARROT SOUP~

Something different, this soup is piquant and sumptuous at the same time.

> 1 Tablespoon oil
> 2 ribs of celery, chopped fine
> 1/2 teaspoon of fresh ginger, grated
> one large head of cauliflower, separated into flowerets
> 2 medium carrots, grated
> Pinch of salt
> 4 cups of water

Oil bottom of large pot. Place celery in bottom of pot, cook about 5 minutes, stir well to coat with oil, add a few drops of water if needed.

Add ginger, stir, add cauliflower, grated carrots, salt and water, cover. Bring to a boil, turn heat down, cook about one hour. Pureé. Add more ginger at this time, and/or a teaspoon of curry, if desired

Serves 8-10

Variations: Serve with toasted blanched almonds floating on top.

~~~~~~~~~~~~~~~~~

~CAULIFLOWER AND MUSHROOM SOUP~

A variation on cauliflower soup, easy to make and makes your cauliflower soup very rich.

Make cauliflower soup as in above recipe, but omit the ginger. While soup is cooking, sauté half a pound of mushrooms. Just before serving, float several spoonfuls of mushrooms into each bowl of soup.

~CAULIFLOWER CHOWDER~

Another hearty soup for a winter Shabbat or one of those chilly spring evenings common in New England and in the rainy season in Israel.

Oil
2 ribs of celery, chopped in processor
1/4 cup cilantro, separated into two batches
1 large head of cauliflower, separated into florets
4 cups water
2 medium-large potatoes, peeled and cut into
 small chunks
1 15 ounce can corn niblets, drained
Pinch of cayenne pepper
Pinch of salt

Heat oil in a large soup pot
Sauté celery for about 2-3 minutes
Chop 1/2 half the batch and sauté with the celery

Add the cauliflower florets and the water. Cover. Bring to boil, lower flame and simmer for half an hour.
In the meantime, cook the potatoes separately.
When florets are soft, purée, add the cooked potatoes and the corn niblets to the soup.
Add salt and cayenne pepper to taste
Float the rest of the cilantro on top

Serves 7

Note: Cilantro is spicy and should be added carefully. You may not want to use the second batch, but if you want some green color in the soup, substitute parsley. Also a pinch of cayenne pepper adds interest, but in this case eliminate the cilantro.

~CLASSICAL BORSCHT~

The quintessential Ashkenazi soup. A soup for all seasons, can be served hot in the winter, or cold in the summer.   Beets can be messy, but they are incredibly healthy.

3 large or 4 medium fresh beets, peeled, diced or coarsely grated.
Juice of 1 lemon, divided in half
Salt
Pinch of sour salt
1 largish onion, chopped, not too fine.
1 Tablespoon to 1/3 cup sugar, or to taste
Garnishes, depending on the season
Boiled potatoes, chopped scallions, cucumbers, minced fresh dill

In a 2 quart saucepan, bring to boil beets, onion, juice of half the lemon, dash of salt and sour salt. Reduce heat, simmer covered until beets are tender (about 50 minutes). Adjust seasonings.

Process soup or blend with blender, but not too fine. Allow beets to retain some shape.

Yield: approximately 1 1/2 quarts

Suggestion: Float a dollop of vegan sour cream on top of each bowl of soup, for color and taste.

~~~~~~~~~~~~~~~~~~~~~~~~~~~~~~~~~~~~~

~GINGERED YELLOW SPLIT PEA SOUP~

The combination of ginger and parsnips gives this soup a surprisingly unexpected taste that is both mellow and zingy.

Oil
2 ribs of celery, chopped fine
1/2 teaspoon grated fresh ginger
1 pound package yellow split peas, rinsed
5 cups water
1 cup of grated parsnips
Pinch of salt

Lightly oil large soup pot.

Sauté celery and ginger together for about 3 minutes.

Add split peas and water, bring to a boil. Lower heat and simmer for about twenty minutes.

Add parsnips, bring water back to boil, lower to simmer, cover, cook for another 20 minutes or until peas are done.

Test for taste. Add more water and/or ginger if necessary.

Serves 7-8

~CARROT-CAULIFLOWER SOUP~

A delightful combination, this soup is as smooth as silk, and easy to make

Oil a large soup pot
1 large celery rib, chopped fine
2 large carrots or 3 medium size carrots, chopped
1 medium to large head of cauliflower, separated into florets
3 1/2--4 cups of water

Sauté celery for five minutes, add carrots, sauté another 2-3 minutes; add cauliflower florets, mix thoroughly, add water. Cover. Bring to a boil, lower to a simmer. Cook until florets are soft, but not mushy. Purée

Serves 5-6.

Variation: Add a handful of blanched and toasted almonds or a handful of toasted barley to float on the top of the soup.

~BLACK LENTIL SALSA SOUP~

Soups can evolve into many different things. You can start with basic lentils and make it into a multi-vegetable dish. This one is a surprising combination, great to make for a winter Shabbat, and leave on warmer for Saturday lunch.

Olive oil to cover bottom of soup pot
1 large chopped onion
3 ribs of celery, chopped
3 cloves garlic, smashed
3 cups black lentils
8 cups water
1/2 cup sherry
1 cup salsa
1 large chopped tomato
1 cup frozen corn niblets
1/2 teaspoon salt, or to taste
1/2 teaspoon ground pepper, or to taste

Rinse lentils well and check for foreign parts

Lightly oil bottom of soup pot, add chopped onions and celery, mix well, add crushed garlic.

Add lentils, water, and the rest of the ingredients. Bring to boil, cover partly, lower to simmer, and cook for about 40 minutes.

Serves 10-12 hearty bowls

~CURRIED SWEET POTATO~
~AND ROASTED RED BELL PEPPER SOUP~

Step One
            2 teaspoons curry powder
            1/2 teaspoon cinnamon
            1 teaspoon cardamom
            1 Tablespoon olive oil
            1 cup onions, diced
            3 cloves garlic, diced

To intensify the flavor, warm a small skillet, sprinkle in the spices and toast them, stirring constantly for 2 minutes or until they smell fragrant. Set aside.

Step Two

Brush bottom of heavy pot with oil, warm and then add onions. Sauté on medium high heat until slightly translucent, then stir in garlic. Cook 3 minutes or until onions are tender. Add the spices to the garlic and onions and mix together.

            1 large red bell pepper, roasted and diced
            4 cups sweet potatoes, peeled and diced (about 2 medium potatoes)
            1/2 teaspoon salt
            1 1/2 cups water or stock
            1 cup non dairy milk-rice, oat, soy or almond
            Pinch of cayenne
            Salt to taste
            1/4 cup chopped parsley

To roast the pepper, wash and place under the broiler. Broil until the skin is charred and black on all sides. Place in a bowl, cover with plastic wrap and set aside for 10 or 15 minutes.

Stir in the potatoes to the soup pot, add the salt and mix with the onions and spices. Pour in water or stock and bring to a medium boil. Simmer until the sweet potatoes are very tender, 15 to 20 minutes.

While the soup is simmering, peel the charred skin off the bell pepper, remove the seeds and membranes and add to the food processor or blender. When the potatoes are done, purée them with the bell pepper until creamy.

(*Continue*)

Return back to the pot and whisk in the milk and cayenne. Sprinkle with the salt and cook five minutes more. Ladle into soup bowls and garnish with parsley. If the soup is too thick, add a little more liquid to thin.

Serves 6 to 8

~~~~~~~~~~~~~~~~~~~~~~

~INDONESIAN ROASTED TOMATO PEANUT SOUP~

Exotic, but domesticated. Don't let the title fool you, and notice that the jalapeno peppers are optional. This soup can be tamed. Made in two steps.

Step one

> Spray of oil
> 2 pounds Roma (plum tomatoes) cut in half
>   or 2 14.5 oz cans of chopped tomatoes, drained
> 2 large onions cut in chunks or thick rounds
> 1 or 2 jalapeno peppers, halved, seeded and chopped
> (optional)
> 1 large red bell pepper, cut in chunks
> 2 Tablespoons peanut oil or canola
> 1/4 cup smooth peanut butter

Preheat oven 425°

Spray or brush a baking sheet with canola oil. Toss tomatoes, onions, jalapenos and bell peppers with the oil and spread out on the baking sheet. Roast for 20 to 30 minutes or until tender. Cool and blend with the peanut butter in the food processor or blender.

(Continue)

Step two

> 4 cups of water or stock (include the liquid from the canned tomatoes, if using)
> 3 cloves garlic, minced
> 2 teaspoons grated fresh ginger or 1 teaspoon ground
> Salt and pepper to taste
> 1/2 cup roasted and chopped peanuts
> 1 Tablespoon cilantro, chopped fine

Bring the water or stock to a medium boil. Add tomato purée and mix well to combine. Stir in the garlic, ginger, salt and pepper. Lower heat and cook until warmed through, about 10 minutes. Garnish each bowl with the peanuts and scallions.

Serves 6 to 8

Variation: Turn into an Italian flavored soup by eliminating the peanut products and using pine nuts and Italian spices.

~~~~~~~~~~~~~~~~~~~~~~~~~~~~~~~~

When the world was created, Shabbat said to the Holy one, 'Ruler of the Universe, every living creature created has its mate, and each day has its companion, except me, the seventh day. I am alone!' God answered, 'The people of Israel will be your mate.' When the Israelites arrived at Mount Sinai, the Holy One said to them, 'Remember what I said to Shabbat--that the people of Israel would be her mate.' It is with reference to this that My fourth commandment for you reads, 'Remember the Sabbath day, to keep it holy.'

Midrash Genesis Rabbah 11:8

~POTATO CORN CHOWDER~

Step one

2 teaspoons olive oil
1 medium onion, diced
2 cloves garlic, minced
2 cups Yukon gold, Yellow Finn or white potatoes, peeled and diced medium
1/2 cup corn, frozen or fresh
1/2 teaspoon salt
2 cups water or stock
1 Tablespoon Earth Balance (optional)

Warm oil in a pot with a lid.   Add the onions and cook for 3 minutes then add the garlic. Cook another minute, stir in the potatoes, corn and salt, cover and simmer on low heat for 5 minutes. Pour in water or stock and the Earth Balance, bring to a boil and turn down to cook for 20 minutes or until potatoes are very soft. Puree in a food processor or blender. Do this in small batches as hot liquid tends to rise.

Step two:

1 teaspoon oil
1 small onion, diced
1 cup corn, frozen or fresh
1 cup carrots, diced small
1/2 cup celery, diced small
1 cup Yukon Gold, Yellow Finn potatoes
        or white potatoes, diced small
Potato vegetable puree
1 cup water or stock
1 cup nondairy milk (soy, oat or rice milk)
1/2 teaspoon ground rosemary (optional)
Salt and fresh ground pepper to taste

Warm soup pot and brush with oil. Starting with the onions, sauté the vegetables. Add the water or stock, bring to a low boil. Turn down to simmer and cook until vegetables are tender, about 10 to 15 minutes. Whisk in the potato corn puree and the milk. Simmer 5 minutes. If soup seems too thick, add more milk or water. Stir in the rosemary and warm through. Season with salt and fresh ground pepper.
Serves 4 to 6

~TWO-STEP SUMMER BARLEY VEGETABLE SOUP~

We tend to think of barley for a winter soup, but it can be served in the summer. Wash barley well by placing in a bowl and rinsing with cold water until the water is clear. Pour into a pot, add water and bring to a boil. Turn down to simmer uncovered until barley is very soft, about 50 minutes. Add more water if needed. Set aside when done and do not drain.

Step one

> 1/2 cup pearled barley
> 3 cups water
> 2 teaspoons olive oil
> 1 cup onions, diced
> 2 cloves garlic, diced
> 2 carrots, diced
> 2 ribs celery, diced
> 1 cup zucchini, diced
> 1 cup yellow squash, diced
> 1/2 cup corn, fresh or frozen
> 1 cup Yukon Gold or Yellow Finn potatoes
> 1 cup mushrooms, chopped
> 1/2 teaspoon salt

Warm soup pot with oil. Add onions and sauté a few minutes, add garlic and cook until onions are translucent. Stir in the rest of the vegetables, sprinkle with salt and cook covered on low, until vegetables are tender, about 15 minutes.

Step two

> 4 cups water or stock
> 2 cups fresh chopped tomatoes or 14.5 oz. canned- with liquid
> Cooked barley
> 1 teaspoon dried marjoram
> 2 Tablespoons tamari or 1 large Tablespoon of Barley Miso

(Continue)

2 Tablespoons maple syrup
Salt and fresh ground black pepper to taste
Fresh parsley for garnish

Pour water or stock into the pot with the vegetables and bring to a low boil. Mix in tomatoes, barley, marjoram, tamari and maple syrup. Simmer on low for 10 minutes then season with salt and pepper. Cook for 5 more minutes. Garnish with parsley.

Serves 8 to 10

~~~~~~~~~~~~~~~~~~~~~~~~

~INDIAN SWEET CORN SOUP~

This soup is a great occasion to get acquainted with different spices. Can also be served as a stew if you let the water cook out, but watch that it doesn't dry out.

Preheat oven to 425 °
Step one:
Olive oil
2 Tablespoons olive oil
1 medium onion, cut in chunks
1 medium green pepper, cut in chunks
1/2 cup fresh tomatoes, chopped or 1 14.5 oz canned tomatoes (drain liquid)
1 teaspoon fresh ginger root, grated fine or 1/2 teaspoon ground
1 teaspoon ground cumin
1/4 teaspoon ground cardamom
1 teaspoon ground coriander
1/2 teaspoon turmeric
1/8 teaspoon cayenne pepper (optional)
1/4 cup unsweetened dried coconut

(Continue)

Brush baking sheet with 1 Tablespoon of the oil. Toss onions, green peppers and tomatoes with the remaining oil and roast until brown and caramelized, about 20 to 25 minutes. Blend in a food processor or blender with the ginger, spices and coconut until creamy.

Step two

1 teaspoon olive oil
1/2 cup onions, diced
2 cloves garlic, minced
1 cup white potatoes diced (Yellow Finn or Yukon Gold potatoes)
1 1/2 cups corn kernels, frozen or fresh
Pinch of salt
1 cup water or stock

Cook potatoes in stock until soft, mix with diced onions, minced garlic and corn. Add roasted tomatoes and green peppers. If you wish the dish to be more of a stew, lower temperature to 350° and return the entire dish to the oven for about 12 minutes.

Servings: 6

~"CREAM" OF MUSHROOM SOUP~

You can use a thicker version of this soup as a sauce for tofu dishes and over grains.

The Cream
1/2 cup white Basmatti rice
1 1/4 cup water
1 cup nondairy milk

Step one:

Place rice in a bowl, rinse and drain until water is clear. Bring water to a boil and add rice.
Bring back to a boil, cover and cook on low heat for 20 minutes or until the liquid is absorbed and the rice is creamy. Remove from heat and cool.
Blend rice with the milk until very smooth. This has to be done in a blender because a food processor will not break down the rice grains. If the mixture is too thick (good for a sauce) add more water or milk until you have a silky texture.

Step two:

1 cup fresh or dried Shitake mushrooms, sliced (about 4 large)
1 Tablespoon olive oil
1 cup diced onions
2 cloves garlic, chopped
3 cups button mushrooms, sliced
1 teaspoon Tamari

(Continue)

If using dried mushrooms, pour boiling water over the mushrooms to cover and soak for 20 minutes or until soft.

Remove from water and slice, putting the stems aside for making stock. Strain the soaking water through cheesecloth or a mesh strainer to use in the soup.

Brush bottom of soup pot with oil. Add onions and sauté for 3 minutes, then add garlic. Cook until onions are translucent.

Stir in all the mushrooms and cook 5 minutes. Sprinkle mushrooms with the tamari and continue cooking until the mushrooms are brown and caramelized, about 10 to 15 minutes. Sauté them until all the water is gone and the mushrooms are browned for the best flavor.

Step three:

21/4 cups stock or water
Rice purée
1 teaspoon dried thyme
1 teaspoon tamari
Salt and pepper to taste
1/4 cup fresh chopped parsley for garnish

Pour the water or stock into the soup pot and whisk in the rice cream, blending well with the mushrooms. Add more water if you would like it thinner. Bring to a low boil, add the thyme, tamari, salt and pepper. Simmer for 5 minutes. Garnish with parsley.

Serves 6-8

~POTATO LEEK SOUP~

An old classic. Most soups taste better the next day, but this soup tastes best if freshly made, so don't count on leftovers.

10 cups water
1 large leek
4 medium potatoes (2 red and 2 Yukon gold are good)
Olive oil
Sea salt

Put cold water in a large soup pot.

Cut the leek in half, wash well. Cut the halves again lengthwise, wash again, then slice the white part thinly. Sauté the white part in olive slowly until it browns lightly.

Peel potatoes and dice
Add leeks and potatoes to the water and bring to a boil. Cut the green part of the leeks finely and add to soup pot. (You may not want to use quite all of it.) Turn down water to a simmer and cook until the potatoes are done, in about 30 minutes. Add sea salt to taste.

Serves 6

Variation: Add chopped dulce as a topping on the soup.

~BOMBAY SPINACH POTATO SOUP~

It goes without saying that this soup is healthy, but it is also festive. Note that the soup is also made in three steps. Serve this soup chunky, or mash with a potato masher---don't purée, because it will lose texture

Step one

2 teaspoons ground cumin
1 teaspoon ground coriander
2 teaspoons curry powder
1 Tablespoon olive oil
1 cup onions, diced
2 garlic cloves, diced

Toast spices in a warmed heavy skillet until fragrant, stirring constantly for 2 or 3 minutes or until spices emit a nutty aroma. Warm oil in a heavy pot with a lid and add onions. Sauté until softened, add garlic and cook for 3 more minutes. Stir in spices and mix well.

Step two

2 cups Yukon Gold potatoes or any white boiling potato,
peeled, and diced medium
1 teaspoon salt
3 cups water or stock

Add potatoes and salt to the onions and garlic and mix together. Cover and cook until slightly done, about 5 minutes. Pour in water or stock and bring to a boil. Turn down to a low boil, cover and simmer 15 or 20 minutes or until the potatoes are tender.

Step three

1 bunch spinach, washed, stems removed and chopped fine
1 cup "lite" coconut milk
Salt and pepper to taste
1/4 cup cashews

(Continue)

Add spinach to the pot and cook until wilted. Pour in the coconut milk and cook 3 minutes. Puree in the food processor or blender until creamy. Return to the pot, add salt and pepper. Heat a small skillet and toss in the cashews stirring constantly until they are brown and toasted. Cool and finely chop. Sprinkle a little in each bowl.

Serves 4 to 6

~SALADS, SIDE DISHES, & VEGETABLES~

"Cooking for Shabbat meals often starts on Thursday night. Since cooking and purchasing food (or anything else) is forbidden on Shabbat, everything is prepared in advance, though making salad dishes or other dishes that do not require cooking is permitted."   Michael Lerner, *Shabbat*

Many diner-outers are discovering that you can make a meal of appetizers, salads and side dishes. This can be more interesting with its variety of tastes. than the main dish entrée.   So too, with our salads and side dishes. You can make interesting meals from the following selection, which will also make great meals for the next day, and are particularly good for spring and summer Shabbats, when you might want to serve outdoors, on a porch or terrace.

Everyone knows how important vegetables are for a healthy life, but some of us were brought up on the standard American fare of iceberg lettuce and overcooked canned string beans, until vegetarianism introduced us to rutabagas, bok choy and radicchio. Today the supermarkets and natural food stores are filled with all kinds of fruits and vegetables, making it easier to get our recommended five daily servings of fruits and vegetables.

One of the most important vegetable groups are leafy green vegetables like kale, collards, mustard greens, Chinese cabbage, Swiss chard, spinach and watercress. Eating these greens on a daily basis provides us with iron, calcium, vitamin A and fiber. They can be steamed, boiled, stir fried, added to soups or made into salads.

Vegetables are practically fat free, completely cholesterol free and very low in calories. They can be enjoyed without restriction as long as you do not prepare them with a lot of fat or oil. That's why we recommend "sweating" your vegetables, which will give them the taste of being sautéed without the fattening oil.

Organic vegetables are always the best choice. You will be supporting your own health, and that of the environment and the farmer. Become acquainted with your produce manager and express your desire for organic fruits and vegetables. Remember that if you buy organic, buy often and in small amounts, because organic foods don't store as well as vegetables with chemicals and preservatives in them.

You can make whole meals from vegetables and fruits. Raw foodists do it all the time. And the Shabbat is a wonderful time to experiment with the concept of raw food eating. There are now several raw food recipe books on the market, or you can access raw food recipes through the internet.

Anyone who has been to the Mahne Yehuda market in Jerusalem on a Friday morning knows the excitement of buying for Shabbat. You can make it part of your Shabbat tradition to buy from your local farm or farm stand in the summer and make your summer shabbat dinners burst with color and flavor.

~~~~~~

"I believe that the religion of the future will be based on vegetarianism. As long as people will shed the blood of innocent creatures there can be no peace, no liberty, no harmony between people. Slaughter and justice cannot dwell together."

Isaac Bashevis Singer

~ROASTED ZUCCHINI AND YELLOW SQUASH ~ ~WITH BLACK OLIVES~

As colorful as a flag. Serve in a white flat plate for a great presentation. Can be served warm (not hot) on Friday and at room temperature on Saturday.   Parchment paper will keep your pans nice.
Preheat oven 425

Step one

> Olive oil
> 2 zucchini
> 2 yellow squash
> 1 large red onion, peeled and cut in quarters

Spray a baking sheet with the oil. Remove tips and bottoms of zucchini and yellow squash and cut in half lengthwise.

Step two

> 2 Tablespoons olive oil
> 2 teaspoons tamari
> 1 Tablespoon balsamic vinegar
> 1 teaspoon maple syrup or brown rice syrup
> 1/2 teaspoon oregano dried, or 2 teaspoons fresh
> 1/2 teaspoon thyme dried or 2 teaspoons fresh
> 8 Kalamata or other brine cured black olives
> 1 Tablespoon fresh dill, chopped or 1 teaspoon dried

Whisk the above ingredients together. Brush each piece of squash and the onion liberally with the marinade. Place flesh side down on the baking sheet and roast 15 to 20 minutes, depending on the size of the squash. Watch to make sure that they do not get overdone and mushy. They should be tender and browned.
Remove vegetables from the oven and cut squash into 3 or 4 pieces, depending on the size. Chop onion in thick slices and toss with the olives and dill.

Serves 3
Note: This can be turned into a a salad by adding fresh chopped tomatoes with a dressing of plain soy yogurt. Squeeze a little lemon juice into the yogurt, a pinch of salt and chopped fresh dill.

~TEX MEX BEANS WITH CORNMEAL CRUST~

Preheat oven 350°

Step one

> 2 teaspoons olive oil
> 1 cup red onions, diced
> 3 cloves garlic, minced
> 1/2 teaspoon salt
> 1 small red bell pepper, diced
> 1 small green bell pepper diced
> 1 jalapeno pepper, diced
> > (or 1 tablespoon chopped green chiles
> > for a milder taste
> 1-2 cups frozen corn

Warm oil on medium high heat in a sauté pan, add onions and sauté for 2 minutes. Stir in garlic and cook 1 more minute. Sprinkle in salt and mix in the rest of the ingredients cooking until tender, about 5 minutes.

Step two

> 1 15 oz. can black beans, pinto, kidney or red beans or 2 cups dried beans, cooked and drained
> 1 cup loosely packed cilantro leaves, chopped or 2 Tablespoons dried (optional)
> 1 cup of your favorite salsa
> 2 Tablespoons tamari soy sauce
> 1/2 teaspoon salt
> 2 teaspoons ground cumin

Add the above ingredients to the pan and cook 5 more minutes. You can end the recipe here or make the crust.

(Continue)

CRUST

Preheat oven 350°

1 cup unbleached white flour
1/2 cup corn meal
1 teaspoon salt
1 teaspoon baking powder
1/4 cup olive oil
Approximately 1/4 cup plus 2 Tablespoons cold water
1/4 cup salsa

Mix dry ingredients together. Drizzle in the oil and mix with a fork until the dough resembles small grains of sand.

Slowly pour in water one Tablespoon at a time, and mix to form a ball. If too crumbly, add more water one Tablespoon at a time.

Form into a disk, wrap in plastic wrap and refrigerate 1/2 hour or longer.

Lightly oil a 9" pie pan and roll out dough into a 12" circle. Place in the pie pan and prick bottom with a fork.

Add the bean mixture and spread the salsa on top.

Bake 35 to 40 minutes or until crust is golden brown. Spread the remaining salsa on the top. Garnish with more chopped cilantro if you like.

Serves 8 to 10.

~~~~~~~~~~~~~~~~~~~~~~~~~~~~~

The State of Israel is dominated by a thoroughly secularized conception of Jewish life, yet on the seventh day of the week, newspapers do not publish, mail goes undelivered, schools and offices stay closed, and buses in most places do not run.

Robert Goldemberg,
The Place of the Sabbath in Rabbinic Judaism

~CHICK PEA AND PASTA SALAD W/CHERRY~
~TOMATOES, BASIL AND TOASTED BREAD CRUMBS~

Preheat oven 350°

1/4 cup balsamic vinegar
1/2 teaspoon salt
2 cloves garlic, minced
2 Tablespoons olive oil
1 cup fresh basil, chopped or 1 Tablespoon dried
1/2 teaspoon thyme
2 cups chick peas, fresh cooked or canned
(drain and rinse beans if canned)
2 ribs celery, diced
1 small red onion, diced
1 cup cherry tomatoes, halved
1 cup of diced cucumber
2 slices dried whole wheat or other dried-out bread
Spray of olive oil

Whisk together the balsamic, salt, garlic, olive oil, basil and thyme. Pour over the chick peas and the rest of the vegetables.

Remove the crusts of the bread and add to the food processor or blender and blend into crumbs. Spray crumbs with the olive oil, spread out on a baking sheet. Toast until brown, 7 to 10 minutes. Stir frequently.

2 cups rotini or ziti pasta, cooked
1/2 teaspoon salt, or to taste
Salt and pepper to taste if needed

Cook pasta in a large pot of water with salt. Drain but do not rinse. Place in a serving bowl and toss with the bean and vegetable mixture. Grind some fresh pepper over the mixture and stir through. Add the bread crumbs to the top.

Serves 4 to 6.

Suggestion: Substitute rice pasta (Tinkyada brand) for a gluten free dish, or for less white flour

~BAKED AND MASHED ORANGE ~
~ AND GINGER BUTTERNUT SQUASH~

Avoid buying a winter squash or sweet potatoes out of season because they don't taste very good. Squashes and sweet potatoes need the cold weather to help develop their sugars and give them optimum flavor. Sweet potatoes could be substituted for the squash. One teaspoon of curry powder and 1/2 teaspoon cardamom will give the dish an exotic flavor.

Preheat oven 425°

> Olive oil
> 3 pounds butternut squash, seeded, peeled
> > and cut into cubes
> 1 Tablespoon olive oil
> 1/2 teaspoon salt
> 1 Tablespoon Earth Balance
> 1/4 cup orange marmalade
> 1 Tablespoon maple syrup
> 1 teaspoon fresh grated ginger
> Salt and pepper to taste

Spray or brush a baking sheet with oil. Toss squash with the tablespoon of oil and salt and spread out in an even layer. Roast in the oven until soft, about 20 to 30 minutes, stirring occasionally.

While squash bakes, add the rest of the ingredients, except for the salt and pepper, to the food processor and blend until creamy. When squash is done, combine together, mashing with a potato masher. Season with salt and pepper.

Serves 4 to 6.

~SAFFRON COUSCOUS SALAD WITH PICKLED GRAPES~

A salad with attitude, made in three steps, but note that this dish can also be made with quinoa for those who want a protein rich carbohydrate.

Step one

2 Tablespoons whole coriander seeds, crushed
2 cinnamon sticks or 1 Tablespoon ground cinnamon
2 whole cloves
1/2 teaspoon cumin
Pinch of cayenne
1 teaspoon salt
1 1/2 cups white distilled vinegar
3/4 cups maple syrup
2 inch piece peeled fresh ginger root sliced very thin
2 red or green jalapeno peppers sliced thin
3 cups mixed red and green seedless grapes

Pulse coriander seeds in a food processor to crush. Add the spices, salt, vinegar and maple syrup to a small pot and bring to a boil. Turn heat to low and simmer for 5 minutes, then cool for 15 minutes. Place ginger, jalapeno and grapes in a bowl and cover with the liquid. Marinate grapes 1 hour or longer.

Step two:

3 1/2 cups water
2 teaspoons olive oil
1/4 teaspoon ground cinnamon
1/4 teaspoon saffron threads
1/4 teaspoon turmeric
1/2 cup red bell pepper, diced small
2 cups couscous
1/2 teaspoon salt
Fresh ground pepper
(*Continue*)

Pour couscous into a large, heavy bowl. Bring water to a boil, add oil, cinnamon, saffron, turmeric, bell pepper and salt and bring back to a boil. Turn off heat and pour over couscous, stirring to combine. Cover bowl and let sit for 30 minutes. Remove cover and fluff with a fork.

Step three

> 1 cup carrots, peeled and grated
> 1 small red onion, diced finely
> Pickled grapes (optional)
> 1/4 cup white vinegar
> 2 cloves garlic, minced
> 1/2 teaspoon salt
> 2 teaspoons maple syrup
> 2 Tablespoon olive oil

Toss the carrots, red onion and grapes with the couscous. Whisk together the rest of the ingredients and thoroughly combine with the couscous. Add more salt and pepper if needed.

Serves 6 to 8

~ANTIPASTO FOR YOUR VEGAN LASAGNA~

This antipasto is the creation of Pam Brown and is so colorful, you can set it down as a centerpiece on your table. Arrange on an oblong white plate so that the colors of the vegetables can stand out. You can also add a handful of toasted walnuts sprinkled with a little balsamic vinegar. No cooking is involved.

Five cooked yellow beets, marinated in umeboshi vinegar
mixed with cinnamon and 1/2 teaspoon of walnut oil
4 medium size carrots, cut lengthwise in half and half again,
seasoned with rice vinegar and dill
2 zucchini cut lengthwise in half and half again, seasoned with Italian dressing
Add a handful of green olives,
A roasted red pepper, if you have it on hand

Serve as a lunch salad on Saturday on a bed of crisp lettuce.

~SMOKEY MEXICAN BARLEY SALAD~
~WITH CHARRED TOMATOES AND PEPPERS~

An exotic combination of ingredients great to try when you want something to impress your guests with. Can also be made with rice or quinoa. Made in three steps.

Step one

> 1 cup pearled barley, washed
>
> 8 cups water or stock
>
> 1/2 teaspoon salt

Place barley in a bowl and run cold water over it. Rinse and pour through a mesh strainer until the water is clear. Shake off the excess water. Heat a heavy skillet and add barley. With the heat on medium high, stir the barley until it starts to get brown and toasted, about 7 to 8 minutes.

Bring the water or stock and the salt to a boil, then add the barley. Turn down to low and cook for 45 minutes or until tender. Transfer from pot to strainer and rinse quickly with cold water to remove excess starchiness.

Step two

> 4 cloves unpeeled garlic
>
> 2 Anaheim or jalapeno chilies, stems removed

Rinse the skillet that the barley was roasted in, and dry. Heat skillet again to medium hot. In the dry skillet, add the unpeeled garlic and the chilies and roast, turning frequently until they become brown and blistered in places. The chilies will take about 5 to 10 minutes, the garlic about 10 to 15 minutes. Remove, cool, peel the garlic and chop. Cut the chilies in half, remove the seeds and membranes and dice fine.

Step three

> 4 plum tomatoes, diced medium
>
> 1 cup corn kernels, frozen or fresh
>
> 1/2 cup red onion, diced small
>
> 2 Tablespoons lime juice
>
> 1/2 teaspoon salt
>
> 3 Tablespoons olive oil
>
> 1 teaspoon ground cumin

(Continue)

Toss the barley with the garlic, chilies, tomatoes, corn and onions. Whisk together the lime juice and salt. Drizzle in the oil, add the cumin. Mix in to the barley, combining well.

Suggestion: Mix in a cup of black beans and chopped avocado. This dish will be unforgettable. If you do add the extra ingredients, you may be able to serve two more.

Serves 6 to 8 or 8-10.

~~~~~~

~SESAME GREENS~

This recipe is delicious even though it has no oil in it. Serve hot on Friday, and at room temperature on Saturday.

> 1 bunch kale or collards, Swiss chard
>> or any other greens, except salad greens
> 3 quarts water
> 1/2 teaspoon salt
> 2 Tablespoons toasted sesame, pumpkin
>> or sunflower seeds

Bring water and salt to a boil. Wash and chop greens into bite size pieces and add to rapidly boiling water. Cook until bright green and tender, about 5 minutes. (This will vary according to the type of greens.) Taste for doneness. Drain well and toss with the seeds.

Serves 4

~TOASTED SESAME SEEDS~

Nice for Shabbat because you can prepare the seeds days in advance and store in your refrigerator. Keeping a jar of toasted seeds in your refrigerator is always handy.

> 2 cups sesame seeds   (preferably the whole brown sesame seeds
> which are superior in taste and nutrition)
> Always delicious when added to vegetables and grains.

Warm an un-oiled skillet and add the seeds. Stir constantly about 5 to 7 minutes, until seeds start to pop, become brown and toasted and are easily crushed between two fingers.

Cool, then pulse in food processor or blender until about half are crushed. Do not over blend or process because seeds will turn to powder or paste. Toasting releases their flavor, makes them more digestible and intensifies the taste.

Store in a covered container in a cool dark place. Blend about 2 Tablespoons with vegetables or grains. You'll have enough for several uses.

Suggestion: Sunflower or pumpkin seeds or any kind of nuts can also be used. Toast in a skillet until brown as described above, except that sunflower or pumpkin seeds will not crush easily between your fingers.

Cool, chop, and store.

~TWO-STEP CURRIED ROASTED POTATO SALAD~

An old favorite made in a new way.

Preheat oven 425°

Step one

Spray of oil
2 pounds red potatoes, quartered (don't peel them)
1 red bell pepper, diced large
2 Tablespoons olive oil
1 teaspoon salt
1 small red onion, diced small

Spray a baking sheet with the oil. Toss the potatoes and the bell pepper with the oil and salt and spread out in one layer. Roast until tender, about 30-40 minutes, stirring frequently. Check for doneness. When done, toss with the onions.

Step two

1 Tablespoon lime juice
1/2 teaspoon salt
Pinch of cayenne pepper
1/2 teaspoon cumin
1/2 teaspoon coriander
2 teaspoons curry powder
2 garlic cloves, minced
3 Tablespoons olive oil

Combine lime juice and salt together. Whisk in all the ingredients. Pour over potato mixture and mix well to combine.
Roast in the oven 2 or 3 minutes to intensify the flavors.
Remove. Add more salt to taste.

Serves 4 to 6.

Variation: Add carrots, parsnips, sweet potatoes or other root vegetables to this dish for a delicious roasted vegetable salad.

~SUMMER BROWN RICE SALAD~
~WITH WALNUT PESTO DRESSING~

Summer makes salad a natural. Have a picnic Shabbat meal out on your terrace or lawn, or nearby park. This dish also packs up easily for a Shabbat picnic lunch in your backyard.

Walnut Pesto
2 cups packed fresh basil leaves
3 cloves garlic
1/2 cup walnuts
1/2 teaspoon salt
2 Tablespoons olive oil
1/4 cup nutritional yeast
2 cloves of roasted garlic (optional)

Add the basil, garlic, walnuts and salt to food processor or blender and blend until roughly chopped. Drizzle the olive oil and water in with the machine running until well blended. Set aside.

4 cups cooked brown rice
1 medium red onion, diced small
2 small cucumbers, peeled, seeded and diced small
2 ribs of celery, diced small
10 Kalamata olives, pitted and halved (or any other of your favorite olives)
2 medium tomatoes, seeded and diced into bite size pieces
2 scallions chopped fine, if desired.

Mix the pesto in with the rice, combining well. Toss in the rest of the vegetables and serve on lettuce leaves or stuffed in scooped out tomatoes.

Serves 6 to 8

~TROPICAL SWEET RICE SALAD~
~WITH LIME DRESSING~

Great for a summer evening Shabbat, or the Havdala meal. Note how this recipe can be converted into a wonderful rice pudding.

Step one

> 1/2 cup unsalted cashews, toasted and chopped-coarsely
> 4 cups cooked brown rice
> 1 large mango, diced small
> 1/2 cup pineapple, diced small, fresh or canned
> 1/2 cup dried cranberries or cherries
> 1/2 cup raisins or currants
> 1/2 cup shredded unsweetened coconut

Warm a small skillet and add cashews. Cook until lightly toasted stirring constantly. Toss the rice and all the other ingredients together.

Step two

> 1/4 cup lime juice
> 1/2 teaspoon salt
> 1/2 teaspoon cardamom
> 1/4 cup maple syrup
> 2 Tablespoons canola oil or fruity olive oil

Pour lime juice in a bowl. Add the salt and cardamom and whisk in the syrup and oil. Pour over rice and stir until well combined.

Serves 6 to 8

Suggestion: This recipe can easily be turned into a rice pudding and served as a dessert: eliminate the lime juice and the oil. Add a generous Tablespoon of freshly grated lemon rind. Spray a baking dish with oil and add the rice mixture. Pour enough soy milk or other non-dairy milk over the rice to cover. Stir in a cup of maple syrup, sprinkle with cinnamon and bake covered for 45 minutes. Most of the liquid should be absorbed and it should have a creamy texture. Check after 35 minutes to see that dish is not drying out..

~WHITE CORN GRIT CAKES ~
~WITH PUMPKIN SEED SAUCE~

An interesting side dish to serve with salad. This recipe can be made in individual ramekins and served as an appetizer, or made in a loaf pan as a side dish, decorated with a handful of corn niblets.

Preheat oven 400°

Step one

    1 teaspoon olive oil
    1 cup onions, diced small
    3 cloves garlic, minced
    1 small red bell pepper, diced small
    1/2 teaspoon salt

Brush bottom of skillet with the oil, warm the oil and add the onions. Sauté for a few minutes, then toss in garlic. Cook until slightly browned. Stir in the bell pepper and cook on low for 5 more minutes.

Step two

    2 1/2 cups water
    1/2 cup non-dairy milk
    1 cup white corn grits
    1/2 teaspoon salt
    1 Tablespoon olive oil

Bring water to a boil. Pour in milk, then whisk in corn grits and stir until well combined and thickened. Sprinkle in the salt and oil. Turn heat to low, cover and cook 15 minutes, stirring occasionally. Remove from heat and pour into an 11 x 7 Pyrex dish or the equivalent. Smooth with a spatula to 1" thickness and cool.

Step three

    1 cup pumpkin seeds, toasted
    1/2 teaspoon cumin
    1/2 teaspoon salt
    3/4 cup water
    1 teaspoon tamari soy sauce plus extra for brushing
    grit cakes
    Spray of oil
    (Continue)

~164~

Blend pumpkin seeds in the food processor until coarsely chopped. Add the salt, cumin, and water and blend until smooth. Cut grits into a 3" round using a cookie cutter or the top of a glass. Remove extra grits and set aside for another use. Brush each cake with tamari and spray with oil. Bake about 20 minutes or until browned. Remove from oven and pour sauce over them. Serve warm.

Serves 6-7

Tip: Use a small coffee grinder instead of a food processor to grind seeds. Dish can be made in a baking pan, if desired, rather than as individual tarts.

~~~~~~

"All animal life and all growing and life-giving things have rights in the cosmos that man must consider, even as he strives to ensure his own survival. The war against spoliation of nature and the pollution of the environment is therefore the command of the hour and the call of the ages."

Rabbi Robert Gordis

~QUINOA PUTTANESCA~

Can be made with pasta like penne or rotini which is the traditional way to make Puttanesca, but using quinoa is healthier and introduces a new taste.

2 Tablespoons capers, rinsed
1 Tablespoon olive oil
1 cup onions, finely diced
2 cloves garlic, minced
1/2 cup Kalamata olives,
  or any flavorful black olives,
                    pitted and chopped
2 cups quinoa, washed
1 14.5 oz can diced peeled tomatoes with the liquid
2 Tablespoons tomato paste
1/2 cup parsley
Pinch of red pepper flakes
4 cups liquid (water or stock plus the drained tomato juice)
1/2 teaspoon salt
2 Tablespoons Tamari

To remove excess salt from the capers, pour enough water over the capers to cover, soak for 15 minutes, then drain.

Heat oil in a heavy pot with a lid and sauté onions for 1 minute, then add garlic and cook until tender. Stir in the olives and capers and sauté another minute.

Mix in the quinoa and combine with the vegetables stirring continuously for a few minutes. Add the tomatoes, tomato paste, 1/4 cup of the parsley, the pepper flakes, water, salt and tamari.

Bring to a rapid boil, cover and turn down to low and simmer on low heat for 20 to 30 minutes, or until all the liquid has been absorbed.

Remove lid when done, fluff with a fork and mix through the remaining 1/4 cup parsley.

Serves 4 to 6.

~BROCCOLI AND TOMATO SALAD~
~WITH LEMON PEPPER DRESSING~

This dish can also be made with broccolini (which is like broccoli, but the stalks are thinner and more delicate), and out-of-season good quality canned tomatoes

Step one   Pinch of salt
                        1 head broccoli, washed cut into flowerets

Bring water and salt to a boil. If the stems are usable, peel them and slice into thin rounds. Add broccoli to water and boil rapidly until bright green. Remove from water and drain. Set aside.

Step two

1/2 cup corn, fresh or frozen
2 large ripe tomatoes, quartered
1 small red onion, diced
1 teaspoon finely grated lemon rind
Toss with broccoli.

Step three   2 Tablespoons lemon juice
1 teaspoon salt
2 cloves garlic, crushed
2 Tablespoons olive oil
1 teaspoon maple syrup
Fresh ground black pepper

Whisk lemon juice, salt, garlic, olive oil and maple syrup together and pour over broccoli mixing well. Grind a generous amount of pepper over the salad. Add the dressing just before serving as the broccoli will turn yellow because of the acidity of the lemon juice.

Serves 4 to 6

Suggestion: Can be made with other greens like kale or collards.

~SPRING VEGETABLE SALAD~
~WITH GINGER TANGERINE DRESSING~

An adventurous salad dish for a Shabbat summer evening dinner for four. It has an extraordinary flavor, and it is worth making the salad the center dish, but make sure you have enough time to make this.

Step one

1 pound asparagus, ends removed

Pinch of salt

1 pound small red potatoes, quartered

1/2 cup peas, fresh or frozen

1 small fennel bulb (optional)

1 cup canned or frozen artichoke hearts, drained and cut in quarters (marinated arti-chokes in jars are too greasy)

1/2 cup red radishes, sliced

1 small red onion, sliced thin

10 Kalamata or other black olives, pitted and chopped

2 large tangerine or oranges, cut into segments

Bring enough water to boil in a skillet to cover the asparagus. Sprinkle with the salt, drop the asparagus in and boil for 3 minutes. Remove and drain. Add ice water to asparagus, just after cooking to keep them crisp.

Add more water to the skillet, bring to a boil and add the potatoes. Cover and cook 10 to 15 minutes, or until tender, Drain and rinse. Repeat for the peas, cooking just until defrosted if frozen, or until tender if fresh.

Place asparagus, peas and potatoes in a bowl.

Remove the tough outer leaves of the fennel and cut off the top. Using a peeler, sharp knife or a mandolin, shave off thin slices and toss into the bowl with the as-paragus and potatoes. Add the rest of the ingredients and mix well.

(Continue)

Step two

3/4 cup tangerine or orange juice

1 Tablespoon brown rice vinegar

1/2 teaspoon salt

1 clove garlic, pressed

2 teaspoons toasted sesame oil

2 teaspoons grated orange or tangerine rind

1 teaspoon grated fresh ginger

Pinch of cayenne pepper (optional)

Lettuce leaves or radicchio

2 Tablespoons coarsely chopped toasted walnuts

Mix together the citrus juice, rice vinegar and salt. Toss in garlic and whisk in the sesame oil, add the rind, ginger and cayenne. Toss dressing and vegetables together. Lay lettuce leaves on a platter or on each individual plate. Spoon salad on to lettuce leaves and garnish with walnuts. Voila! Enjoy

Serves 4.

Suggestion: You can substitute fresh peas for the asparagus.

~MEDITERRANEAN CARROT SALAD WITH TOFU FETA~

Umeboshi paste may seem expensive, but remember that you only have to use a little to produce a big taste. This salad can be made with or without the Tofu feta.

Step one

1 Tablespoon capers, rinsed and soaked for 15 minutes, then rinsed again.
15 Kalamata olives, pitted and sliced in half
1/4 cup parsley
1 Tablespoon fresh cilantro, chopped (optional)

Bring water and salt to a boil. Add carrots and cook until tender, about 5 to 8 minutes, then drain. Toss the carrots with the above ingredients.

Step two

2 Tablespoons fresh lemon juice
1 teaspoon umeboshi plum vinegar
1/2 teaspoon salt
1 teaspoon tamari
2 Tablespoons olive oil
1/2 teaspoon ground cumin
1/2 teaspoon. ground coriander
1 teaspoon freshly ground black pepper

Whisk together and pour over carrots.

Tofu Feta
1/2 pound extra firm tofu, squeezed of excess water
2 Tablespoons white vinegar
1 Tablespoon mellow light miso
1 teaspoon nutritional yeast
1 teaspoon garlic, crushed
2 teaspoons olive oil
1 Tablespoon lemon juice

(Continue)

Cut tofu in half and squeeze to remove excess water with a strainer underneath to catch any tofu that falls. Crumble tofu with your hands or a fork and combine thoroughly with all of the other ingredients. Toss with carrots right before serving.

Tip: Make tofu feta a day or two before using. Make extra--it is good in any salad.

Serves 4 to 6.

~~~~~~~

~TANGY KALE SALAD~

The longer this marinates, the better it tastes. Note that this raw recipe requires no cooking.

1 bunch kale, washed and cut into bite size pieces
2 carrots, peeled and cut into thin strips
1/4 head green cabbage, sliced thin
1 small red onion, sliced thin
1 small red bell pepper, seeds and membranes removed, sliced in thin strips

Toss together.

1/4 cup Braggs Liquid Aminos
1/2 cup lemon or orange juice
1 teaspoon umeboshi vinegar (optional)
1 clove garlic, minced
2 Tablespoons toasted sesame oil
1 teaspoon finely grated ginger

Whisk the above ingredients together and pour over the kale and vegetable combination. Marinate for at least 2 hours stirring frequently. The kale should look limp when it is ready.

Serves 6.

~CUCUMBER AND CANTALOUPE SALAD~
~WITH LEMON DRESSING~

This may sound like an unusual combination, but cucumbers are in the same family as melons, so the combination is not that unusual. You can also try honeydew melon or honeydew, but the recipe is best when melons are in season.

1 small ripe cantaloupe, peeled and cubed in bite size pieces
3 cucumbers, sliced lengthwise and quartered
1 small red onion, sliced thin
1 jalapeno chili, finely diced (optional)

Mix the above ingredients together.

1/4 cup lemon juice mixed with 1 teaspoon grated lemon rind
1/2 teaspoon salt
1 Tablespoon rice or maple syrup or other liquid sweetener
2 Tablespoons olive oil

Whisk all of the liquid ingredients together and pour over cucumbers and melons.

Serves 4 to 6

Suggestion: Add chopped peppery greens such as watercress, arugula or dandelion greens.

~~~~~~~~~~~~~~~

"Shabbat is for appreciation, for receptivity, for wonder"

Michael Lerner, Shabbat

~ROASTED HERB CAULIFLOWER~

There isn't a vegetable that we used to think of as "staid" and boring when we were young, that can't be transformed--like the frog into a prince. Cauliflower is definitely a prince here.

Preheat the oven 400°

2 Tablespoons olive oil
1 teaspoon salt--or to taste
1/2 teaspoon oregano
1/2 teaspoon thyme
2 cloves garlic, minced

Toss the above ingredients together.

Spray of olive oil
1 large head of cauliflower, cut into flowerets
1 medium red bell pepper, sliced into thin strips

Spray or brush a baking sheet with oil. Toss the cauliflower and bell pepper with the herb mixture and salt and spread out in an even layer on the baking sheet. Roast, stirring occasionally, until the cauliflower is brown and crunchy, about 25 to 30 minute.

Serves 6-8

Suggestion: Roast a large carrot cut in inch chunks and add. Also add 1/2 teaspoon curry or turmeric for color and taste.

~CURRIED TEMPEH SALAD~

A good way to mix proteins with greens. Serve on a large platter for lunch for Saturday lunch, decorated with radishes and olives. Or cut tempeh in medium dice, serve with toothpicks as an appetizer.

1 8 ounce package tempeh, any flavor,
Eggless mayonnaise, (Vegenaise suggested) as needed
1 shredded carrot
2 scallions, chopped
Handful fresh chopped parsley, or 1 Tablespoon dried parsley
1 Tablespoon capers or organic pickle relish
2 teaspoons curry powder

Steam the tempeh for 20 minutes. For more flavor,. lightly sauté after steaming. Let cool, chop into small dice, then add all remaining ingredients. Chill before serving.

~~~~~~~~~~

~JICAMA AND CARROTS~

Too simple to be believed

1 large jicama, peeled, and chopped in food processor
1 large or 2 small carrots, cleaned and chopped in food processor
2 Tablespoons sesame oil
1-1/2 teaspoons rice vinegar

That's it. Mix it all together. If you want to complicate things, add a tomato cut in eighths.

Serves 5-6

~SWEET AUTUMN TEMPEH SALAD~

A Waldorf salad with the addition of tempeh.

1 8 ounce package tempeh, any flavor
Eggless mayonnaise, as needed
1 chopped red apple (if organic, leave on the skin)
1/3 cup raisins
1 rib of celery, chopped
1 cup chopped walnuts or pecans
A few drops of fresh lemon juice

Steam the tempeh for 20 minutes. Let cool, chop into small dice, then add all remaining ingredients. Chill before serving.

~~~~~~~~~

~AVOCADO AND ARUGULA FOR EIGHT~

4 avocados
juice from fresh lemon
1 cup arugula chopped
1 Tablespoon olive oil

Peel avocado and scoop out pit
Cut in large chunks
Drizzle with lemon juice to keep avocado from discoloring
Mix with arugula
Drizzle olive oil over the top and mix again.

Note: For a different taste, add a few flakes of red pepper or a pinch of cayenne pepper. Also, a few pimento or red or yellow or orange pepper strips could be added for taste and color. Just make sure you don't overwhelm the avocado.

~MAPLE-MUSTARD VINAIGRETTE SALAD DRESSING~
~FOR SWEET POTATOES and PECAN NUTS~

A great taste for anyone looking for a change in the taste of salad dressings. Wonderful for summer evening Shabbats with a large dinner crowd.

1 Tablespoon maple syrup
2 Tablespoons red-wine vinegar
2 teaspoons Dijon mustard
Salt and pepper to taste
1/2 cup vegetable oil

Up to 3 days ahead: To prepare vinaigrette, mix maple syrup, vinegar, mustard, salt, and pepper in a bowl. When salt is dissolved, stir in oil; do not over-mix. Refrigerate.

1 day ahead, or in the morning: peel and cube sweet potatoes. Toss potato cubes with oil, salt, pepper, and ginger. Divide potatoes between two 9 X 13 roasting pans. Do not crowd, or potatoes won't roast properly.

Roast at 450° for 15 minutes, stir, then roast an additional 10 to 15 minutes, until they begin to turn golden, and are slightly soft to the touch. Leave in pans and cool to room temperature. Refrigerate overnight in covered container.

Coarsely chop pecans and toast in skillet over medium heat until lightly browned, about 7 minutes. Cool and set aside at room temperature until you're ready to assemble the salad.

For an attractive presentation, put spinach in a large salad bowl. Remove cooled sweet potato cubes from pans and layer on top of spinach. Pour dried cranberries over potatoes, then pecans. Sprinkle with vegan feta cheese. Serve dressing next to salad.

Yield: 12 to 16 servings

Note: You may want to double the amount of the vinaigrette dressing.

~LENTIL-WALNUT PATE´~

This is one of our classic recipes from *The Jewish Vegetarian Year Cookbook,* where it was called Moc Chopped Liver. Reference to "liver" was used to indicate familiarity with a traditional Jewish dish, but the word is now unpopular. This paté is similar to the Tofu-Walnut paté, but may be preferred by people who are allergic to tofu, and who prefer the great health benefits of lentils. Incredibly delicious and sure to be a favorite for other holidays as well. Can be prepared the day before.

1/2 package brown lentils (1/2 pound)
1 large diced onion
1 cup chopped walnuts
1/2 Tablespoon tamari, or to taste

Put lentils in a 2 or 3 quart pot, and cover with water. Use water sparingly so that lentils absorb all the water. More water can be added as needed. Bring water to a boil, partially cover and simmer for about about 45 minutes. Check to make sure water has not boiled off, and add water as needed.

Sauté onions slowly until lightly golden and tender.
Put lentils, walnuts and onions in food processor, purée until slightly coarse. Salt to taste. Chill about 2 hours. Serve with crackers or rye bread, or on lettuce leaves.

~CHICKENLESS CHICKEN SALAD~

Adapted from a recipe from the outstanding vegan chef, Maribeth Abrams of *Delicious Adventures*. She has the salad version, we changed this into a spread---delicious either way. Here are two other versions from Maribeth for you to try.

1 8 ounce package tempeh, any flavor
Eggless mayonnaise, as needed (Vegenaise® recommended)
2 scallions, chopped
1-2 ribs of celery, chopped
1 carrot, shredded
Handful chopped fresh parsley, or 1 Tablespoon dried
2 teaspoons poultry seasoning
1/2 teaspoon good yellow mustard

Steam the tempeh for 20 minutes. Let cool, whirl with other ingredients in food processor.
For the salad version, chop the tempeh into small dice, process the other ingredients and mix together with a fork.

Make Food Fun to Look At

~TOFU NO EGG SALAD~
Photo on Page 178

This does not taste exactly like egg salad, but offers the same satisfaction as egg salad, without cholesterol or saturated fat. Use organic ingredients for a special plus taste. It makes great leftovers for lunch on Saturday. Can be stuffed in slightly cooked green or red peppers for a colorful effect. Very good as an appetizer, served with crackers.

I pound of firm tofu (don't use silken tofu)
1/2 cup each finely diced red onion and celery
(or coarsely ground in food processor)
1/2 teaspoon turmeric
1/2 teaspoon Herbamare ® seasoning
1/2 teaspoon dry mustard
3 Tablespoons Vegenaise mayonnaise
1 teaspoon of dijon mustard
2 Tablespoons organic sweet pickle relish
1 carrot shredded

Open, drain tofu, rinse off, pat dry. Steam for 15 minutes. Put on a plate and press something heavy on it to remove excess water. You can also wrap it in a paper towel and squeeze out some water too. Then put in a bowl, mash with a fork.

Add the other ingredients in order, mixing with a fork after each ingredient. Or mix in food processor. The turmeric gives it the "right" color and adds to the flavor.

Chill in a bowl. Then place olives, celery leaves, shredded carrots, cherry tomatoes or other vegetable garnish for a good presentation. You can also sprinkle a bit of paprika on top.

Note: A Few Words About the Ingredients
Use regular not silken style tofu. If you can find tofu made by a local company, buy it. The Bridge tofu is very good and is available at many health food stores, but not everywhere.

~PARSNIP LOAF WITH BROWN RICE SYRUP~

Parsnip is an overlooked, healthy root vegetable with a sweet nutty flavor. The following is a really simple dish. Choose medium size parsnips, not huge roots. Scrape or scrub clean.

Heat oven 375°

2 cups chopped or shredded parsnip
1-2 Tablespoons brown rice honey or agave
1/2 teaspoon grated fresh ginger root or 1 teaspoon ginger powder
Oil for approximately 4 X 7 loaf pan

Mix all ingredients, oil loaf pan, press mixture into oiled loaf pan. Bake for about 20 minutes. Cut in squares.

Serves 8

~~~~~~~~~~~~~~~~~~~

Lekhah Dodi Hymn is the most beloved song for Shabbat

It was made famous by the Kabbalists, who would sing it to welcome the Shabbat. Many would go out into a field and sing this song as the sun set in the sky.

Enter, O bride, Enter
Enter, O bride, the Sabbath Queen

~OVEN-BAKED LEEKS~

Leeks are a great discovery to cook with: they add flavor to almost any dish and will often remove the necessity for salt. The only problem with leeks is that they are a nuisance to clean. Dirt gets down inside the tightly wound leaves, and needs strong flushing with water. This recipe is incredibly easy to make---except for the cleaning, but worth it: the dish requires no seasoning, and is a great accompaniment to meatless loafs.

2-3 medium size leeks
2 Tablespoons olive oil

Heat oven 350°
Wash leeks carefully by slitting each leek down its length. Spread the leaves and wash with forcefully running water.
Lightly oil a casserole
Cut leeks in quarters lengthwise, and then in half.
Place in rectangular or oval casserole dish, lightly sprinkle oil over the leeks, cover, bake 20-25 minutes.

Serves 5-6

Note: When cooked or baked, leeks will wilt to half their size.

Variation: Clean and quarter three or four medium size new or red potatoes, bed them among the leek leaves, let them cook and brown with the leeks. They will soak up the flavor of the leeks. This gives you a vegetable and a carbohydrate in one dish.

~TERIYAKI TEMPEH SALAD ~
~WITH   PORTABELLO MUSHROOMS~

Here is a salad that could be an entrée, especially for a summer Shabbat. For a more intense flavor, marinade mushrooms and tempeh for about an hour before cooking. Use your favorite marinade, or tamari sauce mixed with a little water.

Step one

> 2 large portabello mushrooms, sliced
> 1 pound tempeh or tofu sliced in medium cubes
> 1 1/2 cups water
> 2 Tablespoons toasted sesame oil
> 2 Tablespoons tamari
> 2 Tablespoons teriyaki sauce (optional)
> 2 teaspoons rice syrup or maple syrup
> 1 teaspoon grated fresh ginger or 1/2 teaspoon ground ginger

Clean the gills from the underside of the mushrooms by removing the stems, and gently clean with a soft sponge, then slice. Place tempeh and the mushrooms in a skillet.
Pour in the rest of the ingredients and bring to a boil. Turn down and simmer on medium until all the liquid is gone. Stir until the tempeh and mushrooms have browned.

Step two

> 2 ripe tomatoes, diced medium size chunks
> 1 small red onion, sliced thin
> Handful of snow peas (optional)
> Pinch of salt
> Sprinkle of balsamic vinegar

Slice the tomatoes and onion. Bring a small pot of water to a boil with a pinch of salt. Boil the snow peas just until they turn bright. Remove, rinse quickly with cold water. Toss the tempeh, mushrooms, and vegetables together. Sprinkle with the vinegar.

Serves 4 to 6

~OVEN-ROASTED BEETS~

Like leeks, beets are a nuisance to clean because their red color runs over everything, but like leeks worth the effort and--again--like leeks, have so much flavor of their own, they require almost nothing to be added. In the summer, look for yellow beets at a farmer's market.

Preheat oven 350°

3 medium size beets
clean and quarter or cut in eighths
place in heavy casserole dish with cover
drizzle lightly with oil
Sprinkle with 1 heaping Tablespoon of thyme
Bake half an hour, test for done-ness

Serves 4-6

Note: Beets are often hard to cut. Clean, then bake for about 20 minutes. Remove from oven and then cut. Turn leftovers into hash brown beets. A yummi alternative to hash brown potatoes.

Variations: Cut cooked beets into smaller pieces and sauté in light oil until crisp, or lay out on an oiled cookie tray and bake 20 minutes until crisp. Or chop up cold and put in green salad. The colors are beautiful.

~~~~~~~~~~~~

As a man rejoices all the days of the wedding feast,
So does he rejoice on the Sabbath.
As the groom does no work on the day he is wed,
So he does none on the Sabbath

Al Nakawa

~CABBAGE, AVOCADO, AND ARUGULA SALAD~

1 small red or green cabbage, washed, cored and shredded
1/4 cup arugula
1 avocado, cut into chunks
1 cup yellow raisins
2 Tablespoons vegenaise
1 Tablespoon balsamic vinegar

Mix cabbage, arugula, avocado and raisins (the avocado may blend in and become creamy.

Add the vegenaise and vinegar.

Serves 4-6

Suggestion: Romaine lettuce can be substituted for the cabbage.

~~~~~~~~~~~~~~~~

~OVEN FRIED OR OVEN-ROASTED TURNIPS~

Cover cookie tray with parchment paper. Use convection oven, if you have one. Serve the same day as cooked. Might be limp if kept for the next day.

olive oil for cooking sheet
5-6 small purple top turnips
Heat oven 375°

Oil the cookie sheet,
Scrub, peel, and slice turnips thin as you would potatoes. Place turnip slices on the cookie sheet, bake for 30 minutes. Turn off oven or set for keeping warm through the Shabbat.

Serves 5-6

~RED LEAF LETTUCE WITH CARROT CURLS~
~AND CITRUS VINAIGRETTE~

Step one

3 carrots, scrubbed well.

Peel carrots into thin strips with a vegetable peeler. Place in a bowl of ice water for 1/2 hour or until they curl.

1 head red leaf or romaine lettuce, washed and chopped
1 small red onion, sliced thin

Toss together with carrots.

Step two

1/4 cup orange juice
1 teaspoon orange rind, finely grated
1/2 teaspoon salt
1 clove garlic, finely minced
2 Tablespoons orange marmalade or apricot jam
2 Tablespoons olive oil
1 Tablespoon rice syrup or agave
1/4 cup toasted walnuts, chopped

Whisk together all of the ingredients except the walnuts. Pour over lettuce right before serving. Sprinkle with walnuts.

Note: This dressing is very good over baked tofu. Add 1 Tablespoon of tamari and pour over sliced tofu. Marinate 30 minutes and bake at 400° until brown. Dice baked tofu, cool and toss over salad.

~SWEET POTATO FRIES~

Many of the things we do with regular potatoes can be done with sweet potatoes, and since sweet potatoes are more healthful than regular potatoes, it pays to do a few more things with them, instead of saving them only for baked sweet potatoes and sweet potato pies for holidays. These fried sweet potato rounds go well with the eggplant steak slices.

Olive oil
3-4 sweet medium size sweet potatoes
3/4 cup soy sauce, mixed with two tablespoons water

Heat oven 375°
Oil a cookie sheet
Slice sweet potatoes into 1/2 inch rounds, cover with soy mixture, and lay out on cookie sheet. (Oil a cookie pan or use parchment paper) Bake for 20 minutes, turn over, bake another twenty minutes or until done.

Serves 5-6.

Note: Quantity can easily be increased, and if you want to be fancy, put a half green cherry, slice of pineapple, or a condiment on top of each potato slice. Do not keep for overnight.

~COLE SLAW WITH AVOCADO CHUNKS~
1/2 head of cabbage, grated (use red and green cabbage for color)
2 carrots, grated
2-3 Tablespoons vegenaise
2-3 Tablespoons fresh lemon juice or mild vinegar
Pinch of salt
1 large, semi-ripened avocado, cut in small chunks

Mix the first five ingredients, add the avocado, mix again, adjust seasoning, vegenaise, lemon juice or vinegar

Serves 6-8

~SQUASH SOUFFLE (SORT OF)~

3 or 4 cups of baked butternut squash
1/4 to 1/2 cup tofu cream cheese
1/2 Tablespoon nutmeg

Purée the tofu cream cheese. Add squash and nutmeg. altogether. Voila.
Tastes like a souffle and much easier to make.

Serves 5 as a side dish.

Variation: Use less tofu cream cheese and substitute 1/4 cup of sherry or
white wine.

~~~~~

~SQUASH TRIFLE WITH PINEAPPLE~

Make above recipe and lay down layers of pineapple rings and squash or layers of caramelized apple and squash.

~~~~~

~SPICY OVEN-ROASTED POTATOES~

You can combine this dish with roasted turnips. If marinated will keep well for the
next day. Let potatoes and turnips marinate about 15 minutes.

Four-six medium size potatoes, cut in quarters
1/2 cup Dijon mustard
2 Tablespoons soy sauce
Paprika

Heat oven 375°
Mix sauce well, coat potatoes with the sauce. Place on a flat cookie dish and
bake 45 minutes.

Serves 6-8

~STUFFED BUTTON MUSHROOMS~

Button mushrooms (sometimes called champignon) are good for stuffing, because they're firm and keep their shape, but use medium-size ones, and all the same size so they will cook evenly.

8 caps fresh, firm mushrooms, washed
1 cup herbed tofu cream cheese
(add a few drops of tamari or soy sauce to cheese for more taste)
2 cups herbed bread crumbs
Olive oil for skillet

Coat the mushrooms lightly with oil, and roll in herbed bread crumbs, sauté rapidly in skillet for about 8 minutes. Stuff the mushrooms with herbed tofu cream cheese.

Servings depend on whether this dish is used as a side dish or a main dish. If served as a side dish, one or two mushrooms to a person, but if seved as a main dish, each person will want about 4. Serve with small cherry tomatoes to make a colorful presentation, and with roasted cubed pieces of tofu, to round out protein and vegetables.

Serves 8, if serving one cap per person

Tip: To increase the number of servings, make more mushrooms, sauté and keep the sautéed mushrooms warm in an oven until all are done.

For herbed bread crumbs: save your stale bread, dry it out in a 200° oven. Put several slices or chunks into a food processor with some Simply Organic All-Purpose Seasoning. Process until you have fine crumbs. Store in a glass jar in freezer.

~LENTIL AND BULGUR SALAD~

Can be served as a main dish or as a side dish

2 cups bulgur
3 cups boiling water
2 cups brown lentils, rinsed
4 cups unsalted vegetable stock or water
8-10 scallions, chopped
1 large potato, sweet potato or yam, peeled and cut into 1-inch cubes,
boiled until tender
1 bunch spinach, chopped and lightly steamed/or 1-10 ounce box frozen
chopped spinach, defrosted
3/4 cup toasted walnuts or pine nuts
vinaigrette dressing (see below)

Place bulgur in medium size bowl. Pour 3 cups boiling water over the bulgar, let stand for 30 minutes. Place in colander and squeeze out excess water.

In medium size pot, bring 4 cups of vegetable stock or water to boil, add lentils. Reduce heat, let simmer covered for about 30 minutes or until lentils are tender, but not mushy. Drain if necessary.

In a large bowl, combine the bulgur, the lentils, add scallions, potato, spinach and nuts. Mix well. Add dressing.

Vinaigrette Dressing
4 cloves garlic, minced
1 heaping teaspoon Dijon mustard
1 teaspoon sugar
1 teaspoon salt
black pepper
1/2 cup balsamic vinegar
2/3 cup olive oil

(Continue)

In a small bowl, combine first six ingredients. Slowly add the olive oil, whisking constantly until all ingredients are thoroughly combined. Adjust seasoning. Mix through bulgar and lentil mixture.

Serves 8-12

Note: Potato or yam, nuts and spinach are optional ingredients. Chill salad slightly, if desired.

~~~~~~

A parent should not teach one's children to eat meat

Hullin 8 4B

~BARLEY SALAD~

Vegetarianism is a boon for Shabbat summer meals. Here is a cool suggestion that will leave the cook more time in the sunshine. The following recipes can be prepared the day before. You don't have to have a lit oven for hours on a hot summer night, not even for the cholent.

5 cups water or mild vegetable broth
2 cups pearl barley
1/2 cup matchstick-cut carrots
1/2 cup matchstick-cut red or green pepper
2/3 cup sliced scallion
1 cup sliced white mushrooms
1/4 cup soy sauce
1 Tablespoon brown sugar, packed
1/4 cup dark sesame oil
2 Tablespoons toasted sesame seeds
2 cloves garlic, minced
2 Tablespoons rice vinegar
2 teaspoons chili garlic sauce, or to taste

Bring water or broth to boil in medium pot. Add the barley, cover the pot, reduce heat to low, simmer 40 minutes.

Transfer cooked barley to a serving bowl and allow to cool.

Add vegetables to barley and mix well.

Heat soy sauce in a small sauce pan until hot, but not boiling. Remove from heat, add the sugar and simmer until dissolved. Add remaining ingredients and mix well.
Pour the sauce over the barley salad, mix well, refrigerate until serving time.

Serves 6
Note: Chili garlic sauce is available in the Asian section of many large supermarkets. If unavailable, substitute hot sauce or cayenne pepper to taste.

~BROWN RICE CASSEROLE WITH PIGNOLI NUTS~

Preheat oven 350 °
Lightly oil an 8 X 10 inch baking dish

1 Tablespoon olive oil
1 medium chopped onion
1 green pepper, cut into 1/2 inch squares
1 large carrot, cut in 1 inch pieces
2 large ribs of celery, cut in 1 inch pieces
3 cloves garlic, minced
2 bay leaves
1/2 teaspoon thyme
1 teaspoon dill weed
1/2 cup chopped fresh parsley
1-1/2 teaspoons paprika
pinch of salt
1 cup long-grain brown rice
1-1/2 cups diced fresh tomatoes (or canned in winter)
1 cup water
1/4 cup raisins
1/2 cup toasted pignoli nuts

Heat oil in large skillet over medium heat. Add vegetables, garlic, bay leaves, thyme, dill, and 1/4 cup parsley. Cook over medium heat about 5-6 minutes. Stir often. Add paprika and rice. Continue cooking and stirring for 1 minute. Add tomatoes, water and raisins. Bring to a simmer. Remove bay leaves before serving.

Transfer to oiled baking dish. Cover and bake about 1-1/2 hours or until rice is tender. Add pignoli nuts and the remainder of the parsley. Toss and serve warm or hot on Friday night. Can be served room temperature on Saturday.

Serves 6.

~EXOTIC POTATO CASSEROLE~

There are many versions of potato casseroles. This one, made with an aromatic sauce from Middle Eastern spices, fills the kitchen with great odors for the Shabbat evening. It can be made spicy or not so spicy by varying the amount of cilantro. Know your guests' tolerance for spice. Chunks of challah will absorb the spices to suit the tongue. A green salad will also cool the tongue.

This dish is made exotic because of the sauce. So we begin with the sauce.

Heat oven to 350°

The Sauce

6 cloves of garlic
Pinch of salt
2 teaspoons of paprika
1/2 teaspoon ground cumin
1/4 teaspoon cayenne pepper
1/2 to 3/4 cup chopped fresh cilantro
3/4 cup chopped parsley
Juice of 1 lemon
3 Tablespoons red wine vinegar
2-3 Tablespoons olive oil

Combine garlic, salt, paprika, cumin and cayenne in a food processor and process until the spices form a paste. Add the herbs and pulse a few times. Blend well.

Add lemon juice, vinegar, olive oil. Blend again.

(Continue)

Basic Ingredients for Casserole

1-1/2 pounds red-skin potatoes, sliced 1/2 inch thick
3 large bell peppers, red, green and yellow, cut into 1-1/2 inch squares
4 ribs celery, cut into 2 inch pieces, cut on the diagonal
Pinch of salt
1 pound tomatoes, cut into eighths
1-1/2 Tablespoons olive oil

Combine potatoes, peppers and celery in a large bowl., Toss with sauce.
Transfer to shallow baking dish.
Arrange potatoes among the tomatoes. Drizzle top with oil.
Cover baking dish with foil or cookie sheet. Bake 35 minutes. Remove foil.
Continue baking another 20-30 minutes until vegetables are tender.

Serves 8

Note: Add 1/2 pound fresh green beans, sliced on the diagonal for a different taste, or green sorrel if available, if available.

~CHICKPEA SALAD WITH FENNEL AND OLIVES~

2 cups freshly cooked or canned chickpeas
1 small fennel bulb (about 1-1/2 cups) halved vertically, then thinly sliced
2 ripe tomatoes, diced
10 black olives, pitted and halved
1/2 cup thinly sliced red onion
1/3 cup chopped fresh parsley
2 tablespoons chopped fennel sprigs for garnish (left over from bulb)

Dressing
1 Tablespoon red wine vinegar
1 garlic clove, minced
1/2 teaspoon Dijon mustard
Salt and freshly ground black pepper to taste
3 Tablespoons fruity olive oil

Combine first 4 ingredients, whisk to blend. Slowly blend in olive oil. Stir
in all ingredients from chickpea salad, except fennel sprigs. Marinate 1-4
hours, depending on how flavorful you want dish to be.   Garnish with fennel
sprigs when ready to serve.

Serves 4-6

~KALE WITH OLIVES, TOMATOES AND WALNUTS~

Joggers like to say, "There's no such thing as bad weather, there's only the wrong clothes." So too with vegetables. There is no such thing as a bad vegetable, just bad fixings. Kale is too good a vegetable not to learn how to do it right. Anytime you can make kale delicious it's worth the effort.

1 bunch kale, washed and cut into bite size pieces
Boil kale swiftly for a few minutes or steam in a steamer until just wilted

1 Tablespoon olive oil
One medium onion, sliced thin
2 cloves garlic, diced small
1/2 cup pitted and chopped good black olives like Kalamata or any other tasty olive
2 Roma tomatoes, seeded and cut into large dice
Salt and pepper to taste
1/4 cup walnuts, chopped

Heat oil in large skillet and add onions. Cook until softened, add garlic and cook another minute. Toss in olives and tomatoes and combine well. Stir in the cooked and drained kale and sauté for 5 minutes. Sprinkle with the salt and pepper and toss in the walnuts.

Serves 4

Suggestion: If you don't have Roma tomatoes, you could use sun dried tomatoes. If you use sun-dried tomatoes, use the oil that comes with them instead of separate oil.

DIPS AND SPREADS

These are always good to have on hand for Shabbat dinners. They can be made in advance, they keep well, and can be especially good to serve with Shabbat meals because---all you have to do is serve.

Several of these are now available in most supermarkets, but making your own allows you to taper the ingredients to your needs or appetites----and it is less expensive.

A special bonus is that all the dips and spreads are great with challah.

An interesting way to serve a spread (if the spread is firm enough) is to place a heaping tablespoon of the spread on a fresh leaf of Romaine lettuce or endive leaf and top with an olive or slice of radish. Easy to do and makes a pretty presentation.

~OLIVE TAPENADE~

Great for drop-in guests on Saturday. Can be kept on hand in the refrigerator for several weeks.

> 1/2 cup Vidalia onions, finely chopped
> 1/2 cup sweet red onions, finely chopped
> 1 3/4 cups kalamata olives, pitted and chopped
>   (regular canned black olives work well too, but drain)
> 2 Tablespoons capers, rinsed and drained
> 3 Tablespoons fresh lemon juice
> 2 Tablespoons extra-virgin olive oil
> 1 Tablespoon fresh parsley, chopped
> 1 Tablespoon fresh oregano, chopped
> 1/4 teaspoon fresh lemon zest
> 1 clove garlic, crushed
> freshly-ground black pepper, to taste
> 2 Tablespoons red or orange bell peppers, finely chopped

In a small bowl, mix the onions, olives, and capers.

Pulse lemon juice, oil, parsley, oregano, lemon zest, and garlic in a food processor for 3 to 5 seconds, then pour over onion-olive mixture and combine with a fork.

Place tapenade in a serving bowl, season with pepper to taste, top with chopped peppers, and serve.

Tapenade may be used as a dip with the challah, on top of a mixed greens salad, or as a topping for rice, potato, or pasta.

Yields about 2 cups.

~CANNELLONI BEAN SPREAD~

A simple, healthy and delicious appetizer or side dish, with a very fresh and light taste.

> I can Eden cannelloni beans, drain, rinse mash.
> zest and juice of 1 lemon
> 1 clove of roasted garlic
> 2 Tablespoons olive oil
> 1/4 cup finely chopped parsley
> 1 Tablespoon salsa verde
> Sea salt and ground pepper to taste
> lettuce leaves
> rye crackers

Combine first 7 ingredients. Spread on rye crackers or roll up in lettuce leaves for a different taste, and an interesting presentation.

Serves 4-8, but recipe can be easily doubled

Add more lemon juice or seasonings if desired. Add parsley and process until well mixed. If needed, add some liquid back in until desired consistency is reached. You may also add some olive oil, but it also tastes good without oil.

Variations: Instead of parsley try olives, scallions, or red pepper, but go lightly on the pepper.

~DAHLIA'S HUMMUS~

This recipe comes from an Israeli friend and has a fascinating, slightly off-beat taste. It is a bit time-consuming to make, but trés elegant for company, sumptuously rich in texture and taste.

> 2 cups dry chickpeas, soaked overnight, cooked until soft, drained
> 1/2 cup tahini paste
> 5-7 cloves garlic (roasted, if possible)
> 3/4 cups very cold water
> 1/3 cup lemon juice
> 1 teaspoon sumac (optional)
> 2 teaspoons salt (or to taste)
> 1/2 cup tahini paste (or more, if desired)
> 1/2 cup water
> 1/4 cup lemon juice
> 1 teaspoon salt, or to taste
> 1 cup pine nuts
> Paprika

In food processor, blend first 5 (or 6 if using sumac) ingredients until coarse-creamy in texture. Not too fine.

To Serve:

In a large plate, put 5-6 tablespoons of hummus and spread out evenly to the edge of the plate, leaving an empty center for the second tahini mixture.

Blend the next 5 ingredients in food processor. Pour this tahini mixture in the center of the plate., and decorate with parsley

Decorate the whole hummus plate with paprika and pine nuts.

Serve with pita bread and pickles.

~CAPONATA SPREAD~

Like olive tapenade, it keeps well in refrigerator.

2 Tablespoons olive oil
2 medium onions, sliced into 1/4 -inch rings
1 Tablespoon brown sugar, packed
2 Tablespoons balsamic vinegar
1 large celery rib, cut into 1/4-inch slices
1 medium eggplant, cut into 3/4-inch cubes
1-28 ounce can diced tomatoes, undrained
1/4 cup raisins
1 teaspoon salt
1/2 teaspoon basil
1/2 teaspoon oregano
1/2 cup water
1/4 cup halved green olives
1 Tablespoon capers

Heat olive oil in large saucepan over medium heat, add onions, cook 8-10 minutes, until translucent.

Add brown sugar and vinegar, cook for 1 minute. Add celery and eggplant cubes, cook for one more minute.

Add canned tomatoes, raisins, salt, basil, oregano, and water. Bring to a boil. Cover saucepan, lower heat, simmer 30-40 minutes, or until eggplant is very soft.
Stir in the olives and capers. Remove mixture from heat. Allow caponata to cool to room temperature before serving.

Yields 4-5 cups

~OLIVES AND MELTED CHEESE~

As a rule, most vegan cheeses by themselves are not tasty, but when melted and mixed with other ingredients, they provide an interesting dish. Below is one possibility, which makes a great relish and can also be used for a different kind of melted cheese sandwich. Spread the mixture over half a dozen slices of flat bread and cut into triangles to make the dish look festive.

1 cup of melted vegenrella
1/2 cup of good green olives diced
6 slices of bread

Mix all together

Serves 8: Allowing three diamonds per "fresser," you should have enough for eight people.

Note: This dish is not good for Saturday lunch, because it must be baked and is suitable if you keep your oven at a warm temperature. Serve right away.

~~~~~~~~~~~~~~~~~~~~~~~~~~~~~~

Hail the just person,
for he shall fare well
He shall eat the fruit of his works
Isaiah (3:10)

DESSERTS

A time to linger and ruminate.
In many homes, families sing and recite the prayers
For the closing of the meal.

Desserts don't have to be forbiddingly fattening, or difficult for diabetics. In the following recipes, we have included a variety of fruit and low-sugar desserts. (See alternatives for sugar.) If you love desserts and are trying to eat healthier, there is no reason to remove this pleasure from your life. It is possible to enjoy desserts from the most decadent to the simple and maintain a healthy life style. Although the ingredients and some of the techniques are different, it is quite easy to create luscious and satisfying desserts. You can never go wrong with desserts based on fruits. You can indulge in the following offerings.

~EASY FABULOUS FRUIT DISH~

Sometimes it is thrifty to buy large quantities of fruit, especially when a fruit is in season, but what to do with all that fruit, Here are some suggestions: Freeze your surplus of strawberries or blueberries, or cut your extra peaches into slices or chunks and freeze fruits for a smoothie.
Or make compotes. Here's one combination that is quick, good, and needs no sugar.

4-5 large good peaches
1 cup blueberries
3-4 Tablespoons water
6 cloves
1/2 teaspoon nutmeg

Combine peaches, blueberries, cloves, and water in a medium size saucepan. Bring to a rapid boil, immediately lower flame, cover, and cook slowly about 10 minutes. Add nutmeg, cook for another five minutes until peaches are softened, but not mushy. The peaches will turn blue from the berries. Serve hot or chilled, with or without soy vanilla ice cream.
Serves 6-8

Note: For a slightly different taste, squeeze a bit of lemon into the fruit mixture.

~CURRANT SPICE CAKE~

Preheat oven 325°. Grease and flour a 7 X 11 pan.

1 cup brown sugar, packed
1 cup coffee
1/2 cup grapeseed oil
1 cup dried currants or raisins
1/2 teaspoon ground cinnamon
1/4 teaspoon ground cloves
1/4 teaspoon ginger
1/2 teaspoon salt
1 teaspoon vanilla
2 cups all-purpose flour
1 teaspoon baking soda
1 teaspoon baking powder

Combine first nine ingredients in a medium pot. Bring to boil over high heat, boil for 1 minute, stirring constantly. Remove from heat.

In a small bowl, combine the flour, baking soda and baking powder. Stir flour mixture into the cooled sugar mixture half cup at a time, mixing well after each addition. Batter will be thick and gloppy.

Pour mixture into the greased and floured pan, spread batter to the corners of the pan.

Bake 20 minutes or until a knife inserted into center of the cake, comes out clean.

Serves 18 when cut into squares of 18 servings

~BUTTERMILK OAT SCONES~

Nice to make on Friday and have them left over to serve for Saturday lunch. In case you didn't think a scone could make a dessert, serve these with jams, marmalade or fruit dish.

Heat oven 350 F°

1 cup steel cut oats (check the bulk bin or available packaged)

1 cup soy milk with 2 teaspoons apple cider vinegar added   (to make vegan buttermilk)
1 and 1/4 cups whole wheat pastry flour
1 Tablespoon organic sugar
2 teaspoons non-aluminum baking powder
1 teaspoon baking soda
1/2 teaspoon sea salt
1/3 cup dried currents
4 Tablespoons non-hydrogenated margarine (If possible, use Earth Balance)
cinnamon and sugar mixture for top if desired

Spread oats on a cookie sheet and toast for 20 minutes, stirring a few times, until they change color slightly.
Add vinegar to soy milk.
After oats are toasted, place in a bowl and add soy milk, let soak for 20 minutes.
Oil the cookie sheet lightly for the baking.
Raise oven temperature to 400 °

Combine the flour and rest of the dry ingredients, mix well with a fork.
Add the currants and stir to distribute evenly.
Cut in the margarine, using a pastry blender or two knives until the mixture has the consistency of coarse meal.
(*Continue*)

Stir in the soaked mixture. Flour your hands and knead briefly into a ball. (Don't overmix).

Place the batter on the cookie sheet and press into a rectangle or oval that is 3/4 inch thick. If desire, brush with a bit of soy milk and sprinkle a cinnamon and sugar mixture on top.

With a sharp knife, score almost to the bottom into eight slices. The end ones may be curved a bit.

Bake for 12-15 minutes. Cool in pan and separate. You may want to cut each scone in half. These are nice when served with an all-fruit jam. If you are limiting your sugar, or are baking for someone who is, this will satisfy a sweet tooth without much sugar.

~~~~~~~~~~~~~~~~~~

In college I anticipate Shabbat all week. Each night, I peer over the Escher drawings that decorate the walls of my dorm to read the poster that hangs above the door. 'Hang in there, baby, Shabbat is coming.' I look forward to Friday afternoons because I can take off the heavy bookbag which has weighed down on my shoulders all week. In its place, as is customary on Shabbat, I carry a neshamah yetairah, an extra soul. As I walk over to Hillel, the wind blows through my hair, carrying away all the burdens of the week. The sun sets behind me and the leaves crunch beneath my feet, and I realize that the most beautiful moments of the day are moments of transition....

Ilana Nava Kurshan, Sleeping Through Sunrise

~CAROB CHIP COOKIES~

Inspired by a recipe from *Vegan With A Vengeance*, this is a good cookie to make on Friday and keep for lunch on Saturday. It would also be good with raisins or half raisins and half chips (carob or chocolate) or raisins and nuts.

Preheat oven 350 °

> 1 cup vegan margarine
> 1 cup organic brown sugar
> 1 cup organic sugar
> 1 banana
> 1 Tablespoon vanilla
> 2 Tablespoons soy or rice milk
> 1 cup each unbleached white flour and whole wheat pastry flour
> 2 and 1/2 cups rolled oats
> 1/2 teaspoon cinnamon
> 1/4 teaspoon sea salt
> 2 cups vegan carob or chocolate chips
> (or any combination of chips, raisins or nuts to equal two cups)

Let margarine reach room temperature, then put in a large bowl, add the sugars and the banana, the vanilla, the soy milk and mix everything together.
In a medium bowl mix the flour, salt and baking powder.

Add the oats, the chips or other ingredients like raisins you are using, stir together well.

Add the dry ingredients to the wet, stir together. If a bit dry use some more rice or soy milk.

Line two cookie sheets with parchment paper. With wet hands form the mixture into balls, place on the cookie sheet and flatten somewhat. Bake 12-15 minutes.

Servings: Three dozen medium sized cookies.

~LOW FAT APPLE VANILLA CUSTARD TART~

This is a versatile recipe which you can use with just about any fruit: Blueberries, peaches, pears, plums, pineapple, cherries, everything except melons. Frozen fruit should be cooked, drained and sweetened first.

Preheat oven 375°

Grapeseed oil*
2 large Granny Smith or other cooking apple, peeled and sliced thin
2 Tablespoons sweetener (maple syrup, rice syrup, Sucanat, or agave)
1/2 teaspoon cinnamon

Brush a 9" cake pan or spring form pan with olive oil. Line pan with parchment paper (baking paper) if you have it and brush both the pan and the parchment with oil. Arrange apples around pan in concentric circles overlapping until the pan is full. You can do more than one layer if you like but one layer will work. Sprinkle with sweetener and cinnamon.

2 boxes Mori Nu Lite Extra Firm Tofu, puréed
1 1/2 cups unrefined dry sweetener
(maple sugar, Fruit Source, Florida Crystals, Sucanot, etc.)
1/2 cup unbleached white flour
2 Tablespoons arrowroot flour (see glossary)
2 teaspoons vanilla extract
1/4 teaspoon ground nutmeg
Sprinkle of cinnamon

Blend all the above in the food processor beginning with the Mori-Nu. Add the other ingredients when the Mori-Nu is smooth and creamy. Pour mixture over the fruit and bake 40 to 45 minutes, or until brown and firm. Chill at least 1 hour or more. Invert on to platter and sprinkle with a little cinnamon.

Serves 8 to 10.

Note: Grapeseed oil is better than olive oil in dessert recipes.

~SUGARLESS CORN MUFFINS~

Make these while preparing your Shabbat dinner and put aside for lunch on Saturday. You will be glad you did.

Preheat oven 425°

1 cup soy milk
1 teaspoon apple cider vinegar
3/4 cup fine ground cornmeal
1 and 1/4 cups unbleached flour
1 Tablespoon baking powder
1 teaspoon baking soda
1/2 teaspoon sea salt
1/4 cup soy margarine
    (soy garden or earth balance are good)
1 Tablespoon each maple syrup and molasses

Put the soy milk in a measuring cup. Add the vinegar, stir and let sit while you mix the dry ingredients (you are making "buttermilk" to make them tender).

Mix the corn meal, flour, salt, baking powder and baking soda with a fork until well mixed. Cut in the margarine with a pastry blender.

Add the maple syrup and molasses to the soy milk, stir together.

Add the wet ingredients slowly to the dry ingredients, mix until just well mixed. Batter will be thick.

Line a muffin tin with papers, fill the cups 3/4 full. Bake for 20 to 22 minutes. Check at about 18 minutes, these should be crisp on top, but not overdone.

Servings: Makes one dozen.

~CHOCOLATE BANANA PUDDING~

Too sweet to think about---just eat it

4 oz. Tropical source brand chocolate chips or any other that you like, melted
2 boxes Mori-Nu Lite Extra Firm Tofu
1 cup maple syrup
2 Tablespoons cocoa powder
1 large banana
1 teaspoon vanilla
Cinnamon
Slivered almonds

Bring a small pot of water to a boil.
Pour the chocolate drops in a bowl that will fit over the pot.

Turn off the heat and set the bowl on top of the pot. The chocolate will start melting after a few minutes. Stir until smooth. It is important not to get even one drop of water or moisture in the chocolate as it will "seize" and be impossible to work with.

Blend the Mori-Nu in the food processor until creamy, scraping down the bowl a few times.

Add in the rest of the ingredients except for the cinnamon and almonds.

Pour in the melted chocolate drops and purée until well combined.

Chill at least 1 hour before serving. Dust top with a few sprinkles of cinnamon and garnish with the almonds.

Servings: 6-8

~CINNAMON MAPLE PEAR CRUMBLE~

Preheat oven 350°

Small amount of grapeseed oil
3-1/2 lbs. ripe Bartlett or Anjou pears, cored and sliced into eighths
2/3 cup maple syrup
1/2 cup raisins
1 Tablespoon grated lemon rind
2 Tablespoons arrowroot flour
1 teaspoon cinnamon
1/4 teaspoon cloves
1/2 teaspoon ground ginger
1 teaspoon vanilla

Spray a 13 X 9 baking dish with oil. Toss above ingredients together in a large bowl. Spoon the mixture into the baking pan.

CRUMBLE TOPPING
3/4 cup whole-wheat pastry flour
3/4 cup unbleached white flour
3/4 cups rolled oats
3/4 cup unrefined dry sweetener
1 teaspoon cinnamon
1 cup Earth Balance
1/2 teaspoon non-aluminum baking powder
1 cup walnuts, chopped

In a food processor, mix the flours, rolled oats, sweetener, baking powder, and the cinnamon together.
Add Earth Balance and pulse until a crumbly dough forms.
Mix in the walnuts and sprinkle the topping over the pears. Bake until the pears are tender, the juices are bubbling and the topping is browned, about 30 minutes.
Cool 15 minutes.

Serves 6-8
Suggestion: Substitute apples, blueberries or dried fruits like dried cherries or cranberries. Remember that dried fruits have more calories than fresh fruits.

~APPLE CHERRY PECAN STRUDEL~

What is a Shabbos dinner without a shtickle strudel ?

Preheat oven 425°

3 Golden Delicious Apples, peeled and grated
1 cup dried cherries
1 Tablespoon grapeseed oil
1 cup dry unrefined sugar (like maple sugar, Sucanot, Florida Crystals, Fruitsource)
1 1/2 teaspoon cinnamon
1/2 teaspoon ground cloves
1 teaspoon vanilla
3/4 cup chopped pecans plus 1/2 cup finely ground
6 sheets phyllo
Olive oil
Sprinkle of sweetener and cinnamon

Warm oil in skillet. Add apples and cook for 5 minutes, then add the cherries, sweetener, cinnamon, vanilla and 1/4 cup pecans. Cook until the apples are soft. Cool completely.

Remove phyllo from the package, unroll and lay one sheet on the counter, covering the remaining phyllo with a towel, a piece of wax paper, parchment paper or plastic wrap. Brush the phyllo with oil. Sprinkle lightly with some of the remaining 1/2 cup of pecans.   Repeat 4 more times with the remaining phyllo.

Spread the cooled filling along the long side of the phyllo in a 3 inch wide strip, leaving 1 inch at the edges. Fold side edges in and brush with oil. Using the parchment paper as a guide, roll over filling as tightly as possible brushing with oil as you go.

Brush top with oil and sprinkle with a little sweetener and cinnamon.

Bake for 20 minutes or until golden brown. Cool and slice with a very sharp knife or a serrated knife.

8 to 10 servings

Suggestion: Add Chocolate drops to the cooled apple mixture for a decadent taste.

~LEMON RASPBERRY CORN CAKE~

Great taste combination for a warm evening

Preheat oven 350°

> Grapeseed oil
> 1 cup margarine
> 1 1/2 cups maple syrup
> 1/4 cup Mori Nu tofu, pureed (see glossary)
> 1 1/2 cups non-dairy milk
> 1 Tablespoon lemon zest, chopped fine

Oil 2 9" cake pans with oil. Line with parchment paper if you have it and oil again, or oil pans and dust with flour. Whip above ingredients in an electric mixer, food processor or blender until well mixed, about 3 minutes.

> 3 cups unbleached white flour
> 1 cup cornmeal
> 2 Tablespoons baking powder
> 1/2 teaspoon salt

Sift dry ingredients. Add to the wet ingredients and combine well, being careful not to over-mix. Pour into pans, smooth batter and bake approximately 35 minutes or until the center springs back when touched and the sides are browned and pulling away from the side of the pan. Cool pans on cooling rack for 10 minutes, then invert onto rack and cool thoroughly before frosting.

Frosting

1 block semi-firm tofu, drained
1 container dairy free cream cheese
4 oz margarine
1/2 cup maple syrup
2 cups black raspberry jelly
1 teaspoon lemon rind

(Continue)

Blend everything but the jelly and lemon rind in the food processor until it is smooth and creamy, scraping down the bowl a few times. Chill one hour.

Invert the first layer on to a plate or turntable so that the bottom is on the top. Brush crumbs away from cake and cut first layer in half horizontally. Remove top carefully. Apply a thin layer of jelly over the layer. Add the top and repeat. Repeat with the next layer, leaving the top plain. Apply a thick layer of the tofu frosting to the top. Spread jelly smoothly around the sides of the cake. Add extra jelly to the sides if needed. Sprinkle with the lemon rind or use thinly sliced lemons.

Servings: 8-10 slices

~CHOCOLATE ORANGE WALNUT TART~

So festive, and so good for Saturday lunches

Preheat oven 350 °

Step one

> Grapeseed oil
> 3/4 cup whole-wheat pastry flour
> 3/4 unbleached white flour
> 1/4 cup organic sugar
> 1/8 teaspoon baking powder
> 1/2 cup very cold margarine
> 1/4 cup firm tofu, pureed until very creamy
> 2 to 3 Tablespoons water
> 4 cups walnuts

Oil a 9" tart pan or pie plate. Mix the first 4 dry ingredients together.

Add margarine to dry ingredients and blend with a fork or pastry blender until the dough looks like tiny grains of sand. Mix in the tofu, then add water 1 Tablespoon at a time. Squeeze a little dough together in your hands to see if it holds together well. Form dough into a ball and roll into a disc. Refrigerate for 1 hour.

In the meantime, roast walnuts at 250 degrees for 20 minutes. Watch carefully that they don't burn, stir frequently. Remove. Turn oven temperature back up to 350 degrees.

Step two

> 3/4 cup maple syrup
> 1/2 cup orange marmalade
> 1 1/2 Tablespoons arrowroot flour
> 1 teaspoon vanilla
> 2 teaspoons finely grated orange rind
> 1 cup dairy free chocolate chips
> 1 Tablespoon maple syrup dissolved in 2 teaspoons water

(Continue)

When the nuts have cooled, grind until fine and mix with all of the above except for the 1 Tablespoon of maple syrup.

Divide the dough in half, roll out the bottom crust, place in the tart pan and fill with the walnut mixture in an even layer.

Roll out the top and place over filling. Prick top with a fork in several places. Bake for 30 to 35 minutes or until crust is brown.

Brush tart with the remaining maple syrup and water combination and bake 5 more minutes. Cool and serve slightly warm.

Serves 8 to 10

~~~~~~~~~~~~~~~~~~~~~~~~~~~~~

We play so that we can go back to work. We love so that we can go back to work. One ulterior motive after another. Living in the future.
We are either tied through our uncompleted tasks to the past or compulsively drawn through our need to complete them into the future. We stubbornly convince ourselves that all we need to find tranquility is to haul a little bit of past into the present or take just a little bit of the present and arrange it for the future. On Shabbat we do not have to go anywhere. We are already there.

Lawrence Kushner, Thinking Shabbat

~APPLE PIE~

Old-fashioned, but always popular. Serve with soy ice cream.

Preheat oven 425°
Step one

> 1 cup unbleached white flour
> 2 cups whole wheat pastry flour
> 1/4 cup organic sugar (optional)
> 1/8 teaspoon baking powder

Combine dry ingredients. This can be done in the food processor, electric mixer or by hand.
Step two

> Spray of grapeseed oil
> 1 cup Earth Balance
> 1/2 cup ice water

Brush or spray a 9" pie plate. Mix margarine with dry ingredients until it resembles grains of sand. Slowly stir in half the ice water with a fork and continue stirring until dough starts to come together. Add the rest of the water a little at a time if the dough is too dry and crumbly. Gather the dough into a ball, form into a disk and wrap in plastic wrap. Refrigerate for at least 30 minutes.
Step three

> 8 to 10 large Golden Delicious apples,
> peeled, cored and sliced
> 2 teaspoons cinnamon
> 1 Tablespoon lemon juice
> 1/2 cup maple syrup
> 1/2 cup arrowroot flour
> 1 teaspoon vanilla

Mix together all of the above ingredients until thoroughly combined. Roll out dough into circle about 12 inches. Transfer to pie pan and prick bottom. Pile with the apple mixture and roll out top crust. Flute any way you wish and prick in several
(*Continue*)

places. Place dough on bottom rack at 425° for 10 minutes. Then lower oven temperature to 375° and bake until crust is brown and the filling is bubbling, about 40 to 50 minutes.

Cool at least 1 hour before serving.

Serves 8 to 10 slices.

~~~~~~~~~~~~~~~~~~~~~~~~~~~

~CASHEW CARDAMOM CRESCENT COOKIES~

Always good for Saturday lunches and visitors, especially children.

Preheat oven 400°
Step one

> 1 1/2 cups unbleached white flour
> 1/2 cup whole-wheat pastry flour
> 1 cup finely ground cashews
> 1 teaspoon baking powder
> 1/4 teaspoon cinnamon
> 1 1/2 teaspoon ground cardamom
> Pinch of salt

Combine together using only 1/2 cup cashews
Step two

> 1/2 cup margarine
> 1/2 cup brown rice syrup or maple syrup
> 1 teaspoon vanilla
> 1 Tablespoon finely grated orange rind

Brush baking sheet with grapeseed oil or place a piece of parchment (baking paper) onto baking sheet. Whip the above ingredients until creamy in a food processor or with a whisk. Mix into dry ingredients and form into a disk. Chill 30 minutes.

(*Continue*)

Step three

3/4 cup brown rice or maple syrup
Remaining 1/2 cup of cashews

Roll dough out into a 20" long by 14" wide rectangular shape 1/4-inch thick. Cut the rectangle in half horizontally and vertically so that you have four sections. In a piece of plastic wrap, roll each section into a 12" long snake 1/2" thick. Cut into 2" lengths. Bend each strip into crescent shapes (it is easier if this is done in the plastic wrap) and bake until browned around the edges, about 10 minutes. While warm, brush each cookie with the syrup and sprinkle on the remaining ground cashews.

Makes approximately 30 cookies.

~BISCUITS FOR SHABBAT~

Great for those looking for a gluten-free dessert.   These are drop biscuits, although you could roll them out and use a cutter; however, the irregular shape of drop biscuits has its own appeal and is a timesaver. Easy and healthful they also make a nice dish to serve with salad. But be aware: in doing gluten-free baking, the Xanthum gum is critical: it replaces the structure provided by the gluten in the wheat--- but a little goes a long way. These biscuits will keep for Saturday, but are best eaten fresh.

Preheat oven 450°

1 cup soy milk (add 2 teaspoons rice or apple cider vinegar)
2 cups whole wheat pastry flour (or same amount of Bob's Red Mill
Gluten-free baking flour and a half teaspoon Xanthan Gun)
one-half teaspoon sea salt
one Tablespoon non-aluminum baking powder (Rumford is good)
3 Tablespoons grape seed oil

For the savory version:
one-third cup nutritional yeast
1 Tablespoon Frontier all-purpose seasoning

For the sweet version:
one-half cup yellow raisins (or dried fruit of your choice)
one-half teaspoon cinnamon
one-quarter teaspoon ginger, nutmeg, cloves if desird
2 Tablespoons agave

Put the vinegar into the soy milk before doing anything else, giving it time to get buttermilk-like. Then mix the dry ingredients, a fork is fine, no machines necessary.

Add the wet ingredients, stir/knead until just well mixed.
Line a baking sheet with parchment paper or lightly oil a cookie sheet.
Bake for ten minutes, bottoms should get brown and the tops should get a little golden.

~WHEAT FREE ORANGE DATE PECAN SQUARES~

Preheat oven 350°
Step one

> 3 cups pitted dates
> 1 cups raisins
> 1 Tablespoon finely grated orange rind
> 1/2 Tablespoon vanilla
> 1 cup orange juice

Place dates, raisins and fruit juice in a pot and bring to a boil. Cover, reduce the heat and simmer for about 5 minutes or until soft. Purée in the food processor until chunky smooth. Set aside.

Step two

> Grapeseed oil
> 3 cups pecans, ground
> 3/4 cups oat flour
> 3/4 cups rice flour
> 2 teaspoons cinnamon
> 1/2 cup maple syrup
> 1/2 cup olive oil

Oil a 13 1/2 x 9 inch baking dish with the oil.

Combine dry ingredients. Drizzle in maple syrup and oil and mix until well combined. Squeeze a small amount in your hand to see if it holds together easily. If it doesn't, add a small amount of water.

Sprinkle a little more than half of the crumb mixture evenly into lightly oiled pan, Use a piece of plastic wrap placed over the mixture to press it evenly.

Smooth date purée over the crumb mixture, sprinkle with remaining crumb mixture and press over puree.

Bake 25 minutes or until the crumb is brown and firm. Cool, then cut into 2 inch squares.

Approximately 24 squares.

Suggestion: Try different dried fruits like apricots, figs, dried cherries or cranberries.

~CHOCOLATE BANANA SWIRL BREAD OR MUFFINS~
WHICHEVER WAY YOU LIKE IT

Preheat oven 350°
Step one

1 cup walnuts
1/3 cup brown rice syrup or maple syrup
2 Tablespoons grapeseed oil
1 Tablespoon unsweetened cocoa powder

Pulse walnuts in the food processor until crumbly. Mix with the other ingredients. Set aside.
Step two

Grapeseed oil
1 1/2 cups bananas mashed well (about 3 small bananas)
3/4 cup brown rice or maple syrup
1/2 cup orange juice
1/4 cup grapeseed oil
1 teaspoon vanilla

Oil a medium size loaf pan. Mash the bananas with a potato masher or a fork or pulse in the food processor. Add the rice syrup, orange juice, grapeseed oil and vanilla in the food processor or blender and pulse until combined. Pour into a bowl.

1 cup whole wheat pastry flour
1 cup unbleached white flour
1 Tablespoon non-aluminum baking powder
1/2 teaspoon baking soda
1 teaspoon cinnamon

Combine the dry ingredients together, pour in the wet and mix only until combined. Pour half of the mixture into the loaf pan. Sprinkle in half of the walnut mixture and swirl with a knife. Cover with the remaining batter and sprinkle the top with the rest of the walnut mixture. Bake 40 to 50 minutes, or until brown and the sides pull slightly away from the pan.

Servings: Depends on your guest's appetites, and-nice to bring to someone's house

~UPSIDE DOWN APPLE CUSTARD TART~

This dessert is creamy, luscious yet easy to prepare. What else could you ask for? Using Lite Extra Firm Tofu creates a rich custard like texture, low in fat and full of soy's goodness.
Preheat oven 375°

Step one

Grapeseed oil
2 large Red Delicious or other sweet apple, sliced in thin slices
2 Tablespoons sweetener (maple syrup, Sucanot, Florida Crystals, or agave)
1/2 teaspoon cinnamon

Brush a 9" cake or tart pan with oil. Cut a piece of parchment paper to the size of the pan, line and brush parchment with oil.

Step two

1 cup Lite Extra Firm Tofu, pureed
3/4 cup maple syrup, honey
        or unrefined dry sweetener
2/3 cup almond milk
3 Tablespoons unbleached white flour
1 teaspoon vanilla
1/4 teaspoon ground nutmeg
Sprinkle of cinnamon
2 Tablespoons ground walnuts

Blend all the above ingredients except for the cinnamon and walnuts in the food processor, beginning with the Mori-Nu (or other tofu).

Add the other ingredients when the Mori-Nu is smooth and creamy. Pour mixture over the fruit, sprinkle with cinnamon and bake 35 to 40 minutes, or until brown and firm to the touch. Let cool 20 minutes. Invert onto cake plate or platter. Remove the parchment and sprinkle with cinnamon and ground walnuts.

Servings: 4-5-- Again, depends on your guests' appetites

~CARROT CAKE~

A vegan variation on the always popular cake, suggested by Veggie Jews in California. **Ten hefty portions**

For the Cake:

Preheat the oven 325°
Grease and flour a 9-inch square pan.

1/4 cup cinnamon applesauce (or equivalent substitute for 2 eggs)
1 teaspoon vanilla extract
1/2 cup Earth Balance margarine, softened
1 teaspoon salt
1 1/2 teaspoon baking powder
2 teaspoons cinnamon
1 cup sugar
1 1/4 cups unbleached all-purpose flour
1/4 cup vanilla soy milk
1 cup finely grated carrots
1 cup walnuts, chopped

Combine the first 9 ingredients, mixing well.
Add the carrots and the walnuts. Pour the batter into the pan, spread evenly.
Bake for approximately 45 minutes. Cool before frosting.

The Frosting:

8 oz. nondairy cream cheese
1/2 cup vegan margarine
2 cups powdered sugar
1 teaspoon vanilla extract
1 1/2 teaspoon orange extract

Combine the cream cheese and the margarine.
Slowly add the powdered sugar and stir to combine. Add the vanilla and orange extracts and stir again to combine.

~NO-BAKE CHOCOLATE MATZOH ROLL~

This recipe first appeared in the Passover section of *The Jewish Vegetarian Year Cookbook*, but matzoh need not be just for Passover. This dessert is so suitable for Shabbat because you can make it a day in advance. But eater beware! The dessert is very rich, so keep servings small. (See next recipe)

4 squares plain matzoh
Water for moistening matzoh
1/4 cup sugar
3 tablespoons strong coffee
4 oz. semi-sweet chocolate
1 Tablespoon brandy, optional
1 cup margarine at room temperature
3/4 cup chopped walnuts

Glaze:
2 ounces semi-sweet chocolate
3 tablespoons water

Garnish:
1 pint strawberries, washed but not hulled

In a large bowl, soak matzoh in water briefly. Drain water and crumble matzoh.

Melt chocolate with coffee and sugar in the top of a double boiler or in a small bowl in a microwave oven. Add brandy, if using. Cool.

In a large mixing bowl, beat margarine until fluffy. Add chocolate mixture, beating well. Stir in matzoh and nuts.

Place a piece of wax paper about 2 feet long on a work surface. Use a large spoon to shape a mass about 10" long and 2" in diameter. Wrap the wax paper around it and shape it into a cylinder. Tuck the ends under, place on a plate, and refrigerate at least 3 hours until firm.

Melt glaze ingredients. Unwrap the roll, spoon glaze over it evenly, and chill again. To serve, arrange on platter surrounded by berries, or serve slices on individual plates with a berry or two on the side. Slice with serrated knife.

Serves 10-12.

~ELEGANT CURRIED FRUIT DESSERT~

A versatile dish that can be served with a single crust or as a many layered splendid cake, made with three crusts with fillings from your imagination. Strawberry jam and chocolate are one of our favorites. Wonderful for Shabbats that fall within the week of Passover.

Matzo Farfel Pie Crust:

Melt 1/2 pound margarine, mix with 1/2 cup brown sugar.
Mix into 3 cups matzo farfel to make a pie layer or crust. Press into a 9" pie plate and bake for about 20 minutes at 350^0.

> 1 large can of sliced peaches, drained
> 2 small cans of mandarin oranges, drained
> 1 teaspoon curry powder
> Candied fruits (optional)

Drain canned fruit thoroughly. (Reserve fruit juices for later use if desired.) It is important to drain and dry canned fruits thoroughly, or dessert will be runny and the crust will soften.
Arrange fruit on farfel crust. Sprinkle curry on top. Dot with candied fruits.

Curried fruit pie can be served warm or cold. If served warm, bake matzo farfel crust for only 15 minutes.

Variations: Eliminate curry and spread almond cream sauce on top.

Suggestions: Make 2 or 3 matzo farfel crusts for a layered cake. Put peaches on first layer, cover with second crust, put apricots on second layer; cover with third crust. End with crust or with a layer of other fruit. Or put apricots on first layer, melted chocolate on second layer and apricot jam on third layer--or substitute strawberries and strawberry jam for apricots and apricot jam. Omit the curry.

Servings: That depends on which version you make--the one crust or the three crust version.

~BAKED APPLE CIDER DOUGHNUTS~

Makes 12 large donuts or 36 mini donuts. It is an excellent dessert to have on hand for Saturday lunches and children with mini--or maxi--fingers.

Preheat oven 400° Lightly grease a donut baking pan with margarine.

1 cup organic sugar
2 teaspoons baking powder
1 teaspoon baking soda
1 teaspoon ground nutmeg
1/2 teaspoon ground cloves
2 teaspoons ground cinnamon
3 cups unbleached flour

1 cup soy milk + 1 Tablespoon cider vinegar
2 T Ener-G + 1 cup warm apple cider
1 Tablespoon maple syrup
1/2 cup Earth Balance margarine, melted (1 stick)
4 Tablespoons sugar

Mix soy milk and vinegar and let sit for about 15-20 minutes to thicken and turn into 'buttermilk'.

In a large bowl, mix sugar, baking powder, baking soda, nutmeg, cloves, cinnamon and flour. Whisk until there are no lumps.

Mix 'buttermilk,' maple syrup and melted margarine in a separate medium bowl. Warm apple cider and stir in the Ener-G and whisk until foamy. Add the Ener-G mixture to the bowl of wet ingredients. Stir the wet ingredients into the dry ingredients until blended. Do not beat or over mix. Spoon the batter into the doughnut pan. (Each mini donut shape takes about 1 T + 1 t of batter.)

Bake 12 minutes in the preheated oven, until golden brown. (8—9 minutes for mini donuts.) A wooden toothpick will come out clean when they are baked.

Roll hot donuts in sugar. When cool, you can dust with confectionary sugar if more sweetness is desired.

Suggestion: Other non-dairy milk like almond or rice milk can be used in place of soy milk.

~CHOCOLATE BREAD PUDDING~

Can be prepared ahead, but needs to be warmed before serving. Warm Friday on your Shabbat warmer, or in microwave for 20 seconds in individual servings. If you are lucky enough to have leftovers, refrigerate for up to 3 days, and warm before serving.

Preheat oven to 325'

10 — 12. 4 ounce ramekins/custard cups, greased
1 loaf Italian-style bread, day old or dried in oven
3 cups non-dairy milk, divided
¾ cup granulated sugar
Pinch of salt
10 ounces non-dairy semisweet chocolate chips (1 ½ cups) or chunked chocolate
1 small ripe/soft banana
1 Tablespoon vanilla

Cut the bread into ½ inch slices and remove the crusts. Cut into ½ inch cubes to equal 6-7 cups.
In a large sauce pan, combine 1 cup of the non-dairy milk, the sugar and the salt.. Bring to a boil over medium-high heat, stirring constantly.
Remove from the heat and add the chocolate. Let stand for a few minutes and then stir until smooth.

In a large bowl, mash the banana and mix in the remaining 2 cups of milk and the vanilla with a hand mixer or in a blender or processor until smooth.
Add this mixture to the chocolate and then stir in the bread cubes.
Let the cubes soak in this mixture for 2 hours, turning and pressing down the cubes occasionally. Refrigerate for about another 5-6 hours, pressing down the cubes periodically.

Distribute the mixture evenly among the ramekins, smoothing the tops. Place the ramekins into a pan large enough to hold them. Place on a rack in the preheated oven; before sliding the rack into the oven, pour hot water into the baking pan to come up the sides of the ramekins half-way.
Bake for 25-30 minutes.
Let cool for 20-30 minutes and serve warm, dusted with powdered sugar if you like.

Note: This can also be made in a 9" square pan in a water bath. Bake for 55-65 minutes. Let cool for 30 minutes before serving.

~HARVEST PUMPKIN PUDDING~

Serve this on a chilly autumn Shabbat--candles dancing, red wine in goblets

Preheat oven 350°.
Have on hand 6 4 ounce ramekins/custard cups, lightly oiled

1 15 ounce can of pumpkin puree (not pie filling)
¾ cup non-dairy milk
1 cup firmly packed brown sugar
1 Tablespoon cornstarch
¼ teaspoon salt
½ teaspoon ground ginger
½ teaspoon nutmeg
1 teaspoon cinnamon
½ teaspoon vanilla
1 Tablespoon maple syrup (grade B has the most flavor)
Hot water bath

In a medium or largish bowl, combine the pumpkin, milk, brown sugar, cornstarch, salt, ginger, nutmeg, cinnamon and vanilla, mixing with an electric mixer until smooth.
Spoon the mixture evenly into the 6 ramekins.

Place the ramekins into a pan large enough to hold them. Place on a rack in the preheated oven. Before sliding the rack into the oven, pour hot water into the baking pan until it comes up the sides of the ramekins half-way.

Bake for 25-30 minutes until the tops begins to turn golden brown.
Cool uncovered. Use a jar lifter to remove ramekins safely from the hot water bath.

Can be served warm or chilled.
Sprinkle with powdered sugar before serving.

~NOT YOUR ORDINARY CARROT CAKE~
~WITH FRESH FRUIT GLAZE~

Preheat oven 350°

9" X 13" glass baking pan, lightly greased with grapeseed oil

½ cup organic turbinado sugar
½ cup light organic sugar
Ener-G to equal 2 eggs (add 4 Tablespoons warm water to 1 Tablespoon
powdered egg replacer; beat with a fork until thick)
½ teaspoon sea salt
1/2 teaspoon cinnamon
1/2 teaspoon ginger
1/4 teaspoon nutmeg
1/2 cup grapeseed oil
1 cup whole wheat pastry flour
1 cup grated carrot
1 teaspoon non-aluminum baking powder
3/4 teaspoon baking soda
1/2 cup chopped walnuts
1/2 cup raisins (golden are nice)
8 oz finely chopped fresh pineapple, core removed (or 8 oz can crushed
pineapple in natural juice, drained. Save the juice for the glaze)

Mix together the sugars, salt, Ener-G and cinnamon, ginger, cloves and nutmeg. Stir in the grapeseed oil until mixed well. Add the carrot and pine-apple.

Mix the flour, baking powder and baking soda together in a large bowl. Mix in the nuts and raisins. Add the wet ingredients and mix together thoroughly and spread in pan.
Bake about 40 minutes. Cool in pan.

Note: Egg replacer does what eggs do in a recipe, but it contains no egg. It works best if mixed just before using in the recipe.
(*Continue*)

~FRESH CITRUS GLAZE~

1 cup confectionary sugar
2 Tablespoons Earth Balance, softened
Zest of ½ orange, grated
Juice of ½ orange, as needed

In a small to medium bowl, cream butter and sugar together with a wooden spoon until blended well.
Blend in zest until evenly distributed.
Add a little orange juice and beat in well, adding more until it has achieved a good spreading/glazing consistency.
Taste the glaze for the right balance of flavors.

You can add more of anything that is needed for taste or consistency.

Note: Pineapple juice can also be used.

~FUDGY CHOCOLATE SAUCE~

A perfect dessert for Shabbat- which can be made in advance and frozen. It is also great for getting kids to eat their fruits. See suggestion below.

Makes about 1 ¼ cups of super rich sauce

8 squares semi-sweet chocolate
½ cup water
3 ½ Tablespoons sugar
¼ cup (4 Tablespoons) of non-dairy margarine (Earth Balance sticks)
¼ cup Grand Marnier (Amaretto, Kahlua)

Chop chocolate coarsely and put in small saucepan with water.
Melt over low heat, stirring constantly.
Add sugar and bring to a boil. Boil, stirring, for 3 minutes.
Remove from the heat and stir in margarine and liqueur.
Let cool 15 to 20 minutes before serving. It will continue to thicken.

Note: Keeps well in the refrigerator and can even be frozen. Reheat gently in small saucepan or microwave for 10-15 seconds at a time and stir before continuing to warm.

Suggestion: For a yummy, fabulacious dessert, serve as a dipping sauce for strawberries and melon pieces served with small dessert forks. Orange or tangerine slices also go well with chocolate. Arrange fruits on a large platter and place sauce in the center, or give each guest a small bowl of fruit and place sauce over the fruit to prevent sauce from dripping on the table. For an unforgettable dessert, add rice cream or soy ice cream.

~CHOCOLATE TOFU PIE~

Can't leave this recipe out. A favorite with everyone, even people who still reject tofu. And wonderful to feed to children because it is so healthful. Can also be made the day before Shabbat and chilled. When has yummy ever been so nutritious, easy and delicious!

Preheat oven 350°

Graham Cracker Crust:

1 1/2 cups graham cracker crumbs
1/4 cup (1/2 stick) margarine cut into small pieces

Filling:

1 cup semi-sweet chocolate chips
2 Tablespoons water
1 pound soft or silken tofu
1/4 cup soy milk
1/3 cup agave
1 teaspoon vanilla extract

Grind graham crckers in food processor until fine. Add margarine and continue processing until it is well combined with crumbs. Press mixture into the bottom and sides of a 9" pie pan.

In the meantime, melt chocolate chips with 2 Tablespoons of water in a heavy-bottomed saucepan or in the top of a double boiler.
Wash and dry the work bowl of the food processor. Stir in the remaining ingredients.
Pour the filing into the crust and bake 30-35 minutes, until filling is firm and crust is golden. Serve chilled or at room temperature.
Serves: 6-8
Suggestion: Decorate with fresh sliced strawberries to increase visual and yummy factors.

Index to Recipes and Ingredients

239